John Vance Cheney

The Golden Guess

Essays on Poetry and the Poets

John Vance Cheney

The Golden Guess
Essays on Poetry and the Poets

ISBN/EAN: 9783337777739

Printed in Europe, USA, Canada, Australia, Japan

Cover: Foto ©Thomas Meinert / pixelio.de

More available books at **www.hansebooks.com**

The Golden Guess

ESSAYS ON POETRY AND THE POETS

BY

John Vance Cheney

AUTHOR OF "THISTLE-DRIFT," "WOOD-BLOOMS," ETC.

BOSTON

LEE AND SHEPARD PUBLISHERS

10 MILK STREET

1892

PREFACE.

THESE papers are by way of answer to questions concerning the power and place, the principles and tests, of the art of song. An attempt is made to outline the "case" of poetry; to run back the record, and select the essentials established by the common voice of the ages. Despite a touch here and there for the sake of unity, or to bring the subject down nearer to date, the fragmentary origin remains apparent. Given out little by little during a series of years, in the shape of talks to young enquirers, the matter is, as now presented, rather for such than for those older, who know these things though they — too often — heed them not.

JOHN VANCE CHENEY.

SAN FRANCISCO, December 30, 1891.

CONTENTS.

I write so
Of the only truth-tellers, now left to God —
The only speakers of essential truth.

Aurora Leigh.

Not winds to voyagers at sea,
Nor showers to earth more necessary be,
   Than verse to virtue.

Cowley.

Let the beauty of the Lord our God be upon us.

Psalm xc:17.

I

THE OLD NOTION OF POETRY

I

THE OLD NOTION OF POETRY

A PAPER entitled, "What is a Great Poet?" contributed to the *Forum* for April, 1889, contains these words: "Of late there have seemed to me to be certain signs, especially in America, of a revolt of the mob against our literary masters." Whether or not the clause, "especially in America" lends force to the general statement, the further assertion that the only way to stay the chaos impending is to set up once more the "ancient laws and precepts," is wholly true. Therefore it may not prove amiss to marshal certain "dictes and notable wise sayings" on the endangered art of poetry.

"May the fools get a little wisdom, and the wise a little poetry!" So, with his keen perception of the world's need, exclaims the devout scoffer, Heine. "It is indeed a pity," he says, "that our great public knows so little about poetry; almost as little, in fact, as our poets." We can readily believe Landor when he says, "Readers of poetry hear the bells, and seldom mind what they are ringing for," but we cannot believe that often the wise fail to appreciate poetry, that even the poets themselves are wanting in knowledge of it, till we learn how difficult it is to understand.

For a knowledge of the highest, the noblest, poetry, the learned Porson says we must have "generous, well-informed, and elevated minds." According to Montaigne, whom Ben Jonson and Shakespeare delighted to honor, "We have more poets than judges and interpreters of poetry. It is easier to write an indifferent poem than to understand a good one. There is, indeed, a certain low and moderate sort of poetry that a man may well enough judge by certain rules of art; but the true, supreme, and divine poesy is above all the rules of reason. Whoever discerns the beauty of it with the most assured and most steady sight, sees no more than the quick reflection of a flash of lightning. This is a sort of poetry that does not exercise, but ravishes and overwhelms our judgment."

We have the counterpart of Montaigne's "quick reflection of a flash of lightning" in Thoreau's observation that poetry "is not recoverable thought, but a hue caught from a vaster receding thought;" while Matthew Arnold confirms the Frenchman and the New Englander: —

"The critical perception of poetic truth is of all things the most volatile, elusive, and evanescent; by even pressing too impetuously after it, one runs the risk of losing it."

The difficulty of understanding poetry is made plain by implication, in curious Cousin's statement of the power and scope of it. "It expresses," he says, "what is inaccessible to every other art. I mean thought, entirely distinct from the senses and even from sentiment, thought that has no form, thought that has no color, that lets no sound escape, that does not manifest itself in any way, thought in its highest flight, in its most refined abstraction."

Lastly, we recall the memorable words of the grand old iron-worker in literature, the brawny blacksmith of letters, Carlyle: —

"To know [poetry] is no slight task; but rather that, being the essence of all science, it requires the purest of all study for knowing it." Again, "To apprehend this beauty of poetry, in its full and purest brightness, is not easy, but difficult: thousands on thousands eagerly read poems, and attain not the smallest taste of it; yet to all uncorrupted hearts, some effulgences of this heavenly glory are here and there revealed; and to apprehend it clearly and wholly, to acquire and maintain a sense and heart that sees and worships it, is the last perfection of all human culture."

It would seem, then, that poetry is not simply hard, but very hard, the hardest of all the productions of the human mind to understand. We can believe Heine, now, and we shall not be surprised to find the trustworthy critic of poetry as rare as the pichiciago. In Cousin's "most refined abstraction," in the evanescence, the elusiveness, mentioned by Montaigne and Thoreau, and finally in Carlyle's "essence of all science," of all knowing, it is easy to see whence the difficulty springs.

But the every-day "dictes" on the subject of poetry, the lesser definitions of it, differ widely from the Caxtonian dictes, from the great definitions. "A rhythmical creation of beauty"; "literary production which attains the power of giving pleasure by its form as distinct from the matter"; "imaginative passion", — the dictes of this sort, while they are good in comparison with hundreds of others, do not arouse a suspicion of the difficulty of poetry. They do not stamp it as a high thing, "the supreme of power"; and these are the dictes that the many read and accept. Hence, while so much is said of poetry, so little is learned; and hence the "revolt" against the masters.

This imperfect understanding, this blurred view of poetry, this indifferent attitude toward it, is naturally, logically, one of the misfortunes of our busy day. In the hurry of buying and selling, of tilling and building, we have lost the meaning poetry had to the leisurely ancients, the importance they attached to it, — the large meaning, the supreme importance. We no longer give the poet and the prophet one name, our muses are no longer "those that inquire." When the thousand-eyed press, prevailing over all privacy, informs us that a singer, in some quarter of our vast possessions, is trilling new ditties for the Christmas market, we do not think of him as boring, as drilling, into the heart, the secret, of life. It is to be feared, indeed, that he is not doing quite this; still it would bespeak a day of better things were we wont to give him the benefit of the doubt.

Let us climb back to the source, and see if from the calm height of the olden time we can not get a clearer, a wider view. Poetry, like all high and mighty powers, strikes root in the rich black soil of mystery. In the old — really the new — days it was deified; the Greek graciously referring its origin to Orpheus, the Northman styling it the "present, or the drink, of Odin." Cicero, with Plato and Democritus in mind, says, "I have often heard that no real poet can exist without the spirit being on fire, and without, as it were, a dash of madness." "*Aut insanit homo, aut versus facit*": here Horace and tradition speak together.

The old ideas of poetry, differ as they may in particulars, converge at this point; viz., that poetry is something beyond, above the man, entering into him at certain times and under certain conditions, and giving him superhuman force of utterance. Hesiod is not enabled to sing by his own effort; quietly feeding his lambs at the foot of Helicon, the muses must bring him a laurel bough, and bid him sing. Lorn Cassandra does not wander on the hills, uttering words of her own; she is simply the mouth-piece of Apollo. All this attributing of the extramundane, of the preterhuman, attests the power of poetry from the beginning. Man could not reach its secret; it was above him, from a source far higher and mightier than himself. The ancients worshipped at the shrine of poetry; it was to them a goddess off whose face, divinely fair, the veil was never lifted.

The old large meaning of poetry was still abroad at a comparatively recent period. The scholar, Sir Thomas Elyot, who died about the middle of the sixteenth century, assures us of this : —

"Semblably they that make verses, expressing thereby none other learning but the craft of versifying, be not of ancient writers named poets, but only called versifiers." Elsewhere he nobly declares, "And poetry was the first philosophy that ever was known, whereby men from their childhood were brought to the reason, how to live well, learning thereby not only manners and natural affections, but also the wonderful works of Nature, mixing serious matter with things pleasant."

Later, we find Rare Ben, of the spacious times, quoting Aristotle to a similar purport: " A poet is that which by the Greeks is called a maker, or a feigner; his art, an art of imitation or feigning, expressing the life of man in fit measure, numbers, and harmony."

It is a pleasure in this connection to mention, among the best sayings on poetry, one of the neglected Blair's: "Poetry in its ancient, original condition included the whole burst of the human mind."

Such was the old poetry, and such the notion of it.

Three men of our time have held closely to the old notion: Carlyle, Emerson and Matthew Arnold. We might well add a fourth, Ruskin. With these men poetry is still a thing of infi-

nite worth and beauty, the "unfallen speech";
and the poets are still "God's prophets of the
beautiful." "The beauty of poetry," says the
fervent Scotchman, "dwells and is born in the
innermost spirit of man, united to all love of
virtue, to all true belief in God; or rather, it is
one with this love and this belief, another phase
of the same highest principle in the mysterious
infinitude of the human soul."

Again, he says that the aim of poetry is to
incorporate the "everlasting reason of man in
forms visible to the sense, and suitable to it."
Still again, he exclaims, "Poetic creation —
what is this but seeing the thing sufficiently?"
Life accurately, sufficiently seen, high truth
fastened in permanent forms of beauty — this
is the old notion. With Carlyle poetry is diffi-
cult, divine; for what is hard and high, what
divine among mortals, if not the right seeing of
truth at its purest, truth in its first, far beauty,
— the right reading of the mystery we call
life? "The poet names the thing because he

sees it," says Emerson. To see, really see; here we hit the very heart of poetry and of difficulty. Those winged words of Ruskin, what are they?

" The greatest thing a human soul ever does in this world is to *see* something, and tell what it *saw* in a plain way. Hundreds of people can talk for one who can think, but thousands can think for one who can see. To see clearly is poetry, prophecy, and religion, all in one."

The beauty of poetry " one with all love of virtue, of all true belief in God," says Carlyle. " The poet, or the man of Beauty," says Emerson. . . . "God has not made some beautiful things, but Beauty is the creator of the universe. . . . The love of truth, the love of good, the love of beauty, these three are equal." " Poetry, prophecy, and religion, all in one," says Ruskin. Is this empty rhetoric, or are poetry, prophecy and religion, indeed, one and the same? Arnold answers, " The strongest part of our religion to-day is its unconscious poetry." And Emerson adds, "All that we call sacred history attests that the birth of a poet is the principal event in chronology. . . . The religions of the world are the ejaculations of a few imaginative men."

Poetry tells us "how to live well"; "poetry expresses the life of man in fit measure, numbers, and harmony"; poetry incorporates the "everlasting reason of man"; — these best of sayings and that other excellent saying of Emerson, "The poet turns the world to glass, and shows us all things in their right series and procession," we find again in what comes, perhaps, the nearest to a definition of poetry: "the noble and profound application of ideas to life, under the conditions immutably fixed by the laws of poetic beauty and poetic truth."

"It is important," Arnold continues, "to hold fast to this: that poetry is at bottom a criticism of life; that the greatness of a poet lies in his powerful and beautiful application of ideas to life, to the question how to live."

Only on this old high definition of poetry can we pronounce it of first importance, "the supreme of power." Only on these great terms could Arnold find the right to declare, "The future of poetry is immense, because in poetry, where it is worthy of its high destinies, our race, as time goes on, will find an ever surer and surer stay."

On the old high definition, the right seeing of life, expressed according to the immutable laws of poetic truth and beauty, we have in poetry a vital subject, the ruling power of man's mind and heart since time was; we have to deal with man's happiness, his self-preservation.

Metaphysics has done its part toward helping us to forget the old notion. It has been gathered down on this bright subject; it has so overgrown it that the one thing first and last to be searched for has been lost sight of. Who but those heavy with the hangings and trappings of the metaphysical armory could strive to separate inseparables, to divide the real from the ideal?

As if the ideal were not the spirit, the life, of the real, the very real!

"The true ideal is not opposed to the real, nor is it any artificial heightening thereof; but lies in it, and blessed are the eyes that find it. It is the *mens divinior* which hides within the actual, transfiguring matter-of-fact into matter-of-meaning for him who has the gift of second sight."

If this saying of Lowell's does not contain all we may wish to know, it contains all we can know and all we need to know. "It is not true," says Channing, "that the poet paints a life which does not exist. He only extracts and concentrates, as it were, life's ethereal essence, arrests and condenses its volatile fragrance."

Again, poetry has been recently defined as "All writing tending to noble emotion, or reflection leading to such emotion, having for its subject mankind or the rational universe, or both, in relation to God, and using for the most part the vehicle of rhythmical form."

There is much in this saying, but is it not erroneous, fatally false, where it makes poetry a thing solely for the emotions?   Still, this saying concerning the reception of poetry is better than Mill's saying concerning the inception of it.   The poet " is not a poet," says Mill, " because he has ideas of any particular kind, but because the succession of his ideas is subordinate to the course of his emotions."

Can anything be plainer than that the right seeing of so vast, so complex phenomena as life exhibits must come of the "everlasting reason " and come to the "everlasting reason " ; that it is a matter of mind and for mind?   Emotion plays its part, but if the intellect ever leads and controls anywhere, it is here.

" Good sense," says Coleridge, " is the body of poetic genius; . . . poetic composition is the result and pledge of a watchful good sense, of fine and luminous distinction, and of complete self-possession."   " Poetry," says Carlyle, " turns on the power of intellect ".   " The sign and credentials of the poet are," says Emerson, "that he announces that which no man foretold. . . . He knows and tells."

"The truth of poetry," Mill continues, "is to paint the human soul truly," it is the "delineation of the deeper and more secret workings of human emotion."

This is a part of the truth of poetry; the whole truth of it is to see man and all that is not man, to read aright, to interpret faithfully, and to fix distinctly and imperishably in blazing symbols, the primal laws, the meaning of life. After all, the poet's originality is in inverse ratio to his greatness. The great poet is the word-for-word reporter: —

"For poetry was all written before time was, and whenever we are so finely organized that we can penetrate into that region where the air is music, we hear those primal warblings, and attempt to write them down, but we lose ever and anon a word, or a verse, and substitute something of our own, and thus miswrite the poem."

For this reporting is required the "whole burst of the human mind," and for the reception of the report is required, as we have seen, simplicity of vision, widened and strengthened by the severest preparation of which mind and soul are capable. The emotions may give, may receive, a great deal, but not all that was written before time was. Coleridge, inspired by the presence of his sleeping child, reports certain phases of nature : —

> " Therefore all seasons shall be sweet to thee,
> Whether the summer clothe the general earth
> With greenness, or the redbreast sit and sing
> Betwixt the tufts of snow on the bare branch
> Of mossy apple-tree, while the nighthatch
> Smokes in the sunthaw; whether the eve-drops fall,
> Heard only in the trances of the blast,
> Or if the secret ministry of frost
> Shall hang them up in silent icicles,
> Quietly shining to the quiet moon."

Are we to say that this marvellous reproduction of nature, this exact seeing, this incision and expression to the very life, is possible to one who has no "ideas of a particular kind"?

Mill's saying that poetry is "thought colored by emotions, expressed in metre and overheard," is far better than his other saying. There is a beautiful coloring of emotion in the lines quoted, but the first thing we see is that the poet sees. Sight does not rest upon the course of emotions, it rests upon the eye. Coleridge sees, he "knows and tells"; tells in such a manner that we can see in his few words more than we can see, standing before nature herself. This reach and compression mean sight and mind: sight and mind so reach and compress, span thought's sky with a single phrase, whisper divinity in a little word. Emotion will not suffice here; much less will it suffice when we come to the right seeing of life at large, in its infinite extent and variety. Arnold says of religion that it is " morals touched with emotion." So we may say that poetry is thought, yes, morals, touched with emotion ; but we can not say that the sun of poetry rises and sets in emotion.

The exception that the old notion compels

us to take to Mill's statement regarding the emotion in poetry, is only partial; but when he says that the poet "is not a poet because he has ideas of any particular kind," the dissent becomes total. The very pith of the old notion lies in the affirmation that it is because the poet *has* ideas of a particular kind that he is a poet; and probably the scientists will only too cheerfully agree with us when we add, the poet's particular kind of ideas is not the scientific kind. The aim of poetry, in the broad sense, is one with that of philosophy and science, — the truth; but the method of poetry is not the method of philosophy and science, nor is the order of truth sought by it the order of truth sought by these. Science and philosophy feel their way, poetry opens instantly on the truth. Poetry is literature; and "the grand work of literary genius," as Arnold's saying runs, "is a work of synthesis and exposition, not of analysis and discovery." Science is slow, it searches; poetry is swift, it sees: this, in brief, is the dif-

ference in method. As to the difference be-
tween the kinds of truth sought, the poet's kind
of truth lies within or beyond the truth that
science toils patiently toward, step by step; the
poet's kind of truth is the ideal, the very real.

> " For double the vision my eyes do see,
> And a double vision is always with me.
> With my inward eye, 'tis an old man gray;
> With my outward, a thistle across my way."

The scientist sees a thistle; Blake, the poet,
with his eye on a thistle, sees an " old man
gray." The two things seen, differ widely, the
two methods differ as widely. So wide is the dif-
ference of method between the poet and the
scientist, that Blake, comparing his method with
Newton's, terms the scientist's method a sleep:

> " May God us keep
> From single vision and Newton's sleep."

The scientist's vision is single, stopping at the
obvious; the poet's is double, stopping not short
of the inner, the central truth, the red heart of

life. Poetry leaps to the ultimate, essential
beauty, the grand unity. *And God saw that it
was good:* poetry never drops this note of glory.
Amid all the mutation and perturbation of
science and philosophy, poetry sees as first it
saw. Science and philosophy may hesitate, may
grope, may despair, poetry holds to the old vis-
ion of joy; it is trustful, it is safe. Poetry is
an art. Why? Because of the kind of truth
it sees, the truth that is always beautiful, or, to
use the old synonym, that is always good; be-
cause of its method of seeing, its leaping sight,
and because of its glowing report, alive and
shining with wonderful words, the perfection of
human speech. The poet's kind of truth is in
itself pleasurable; his manner of report is cor-
respondingly pleasurable, stimulative of joy.

"Pleasure is not indispensable," says Lessing.
It depends on the kind of pleasure. The high
pleasure of the poet's kind of truth *is* indispen-
sable; whatever else men let go they cling to
this. The Happy Isles are distant, science does

not carry that far; only poetry can safely make the long, difficult journey. There is a homely old saying, "The plaster must be as broad as the sore." We are not at ease, we are hurt by the world. Science applies its strip, varying in breadth from year to year, but the wound is not covered. We must apply the "best part of our religion," the balm of poetry, the joy announced so long ago, — *And God saw that it was good.* Mill, finding that the poet has no "ideas of a particular kind," may consistently find Wordsworth's poetry no more than the poetry of culture. We that believe a poet to have ideas of a particular kind, and of the most exalted kind, find Wordsworth a born seer, important, immortal; he has the old note of glory. This, not the part played by the emotions, is the vital thing to discover; and the longer we speculate upon the emotions, the longer is the discovery delayed: reasoning too much, we fail to see.

The old notion makes the perception of truth

the immediate object of the highest poetry. Here we are confronted by eminent authorities, among them Coleridge.

" A poem," he says, " is that species of composition which is opposed to works of science, by proposing for its immediate object pleasure, not truth."

In his remarks on Wordsworth, this statement is reaffirmed: Wordsworth's work destroys the " main, fundamental distinction, not only between a poem and prose, but even between philosophy and works of fiction, inasmuch as it proposes *truth* for its immediate object instead of *pleasure*."

Coleridge opposes poetry to science. So far he is with us; we divide ways when it comes to the cause of the opposition. We have endeavored to show that the cause of the opposition lies in the kind of truth sought. Whether it lie here, or in the relative positions of truth and pleasure, will be easier of decision, perhaps, when we get farther along. As to

trenching on the ground of the moral philoso-
pher by putting truth first, how can a poet do
this? Poetry has for its aim the moral, the
good, the beautiful; poetry is also philosophic.
"Poetry is the first philosophy that ever was
known." To this we add Coleridge's own
words: "No man was ever yet a great poet,
without being at the same time a profound
philosopher." But while the poet is a moral
philosopher, it must not be forgotten that he is
first a seer; employing the method of the seer,
the instantaneous method, the method of
beauty. Here is the difference, the difference
of method. We do not see how the poet can
trench on the ground of the moral philosopher;
for this ground is the poet's by first occupancy.
"There are, indeed, both in Arabic and Per-
sian," says Sir William Jones, "philosophical
tracts on ethics, written with sound ratioci-
nation and elegant perspicuity; but in every
part of the Eastern world, from Pekin to
Damascus, the popular teachers of moral wis-

dom have immemorially been poets, and there would be no end of enumerating their works, which are still extant in the five principal languages of Asia."

Neither, indeed, do we see how the poet can trench on the method of the moral philosopher; for the instant he does this he is no longer a poet.

But is Coleridge flatly against us? "Now," he says, continuing his remarks on Wordsworth, " till the blessed time shall come when truth itself shall be pleasure, and both shall be so united as to be distinguishable in words only, not in feeling, it will remain the poet's office to proceed upon that state of association which actually exists in general, instead of attempting first to make it what it ought to be, and then to let the pleasure follow."

All poetry gives pleasure, and the pleasure rises in kind and degree with the kind and degree of the poetry. We speak of the highest poetry, therefore of the highest pleasure; and has not the time come when high poetic truth and high pleasure are inseparable? Keats says, "Beauty is truth, truth is beauty"; and what other power is so potent for pleasure as beauty? It was on the trinity of truth, beauty, and pleasure that Keats built, and built lastingly. The truth of science cannot give the pleasure under consideration, neither can the truth of philosophy, these being put as the scientist and the philosopher put them; but put as the poet puts them, they must yield pleasure; while the truth of the poet, as uttered by him, must yield the highest pleasure, the pleasure being twin-born with the truth. The poet's truth and expression form a perfect whole of beauty, and a whole of beauty "is a joy."

Again, Coleridge makes an admission which we will set against his formal declaration regarding truth and pleasure. He says: "The first chapter of Isaiah (indeed, a very large proportion of the whole book), is poetry

in the most emphatic sense; yet it would not
be less irrational than strange to assert that
pleasure, and not truth, was the immediate
object of the prophet."

Finally, we add Coleridge's lines to Words-
worth : —

"Of Truth profound, a sweet, continuous lay,
    Not learnt, but native, her own natural notes."

Coleridge, the poet, sees clearer than Cole-
ridge, the metaphysician. "Truth's own natu-
ral notes" — these indeed Wordsworth's are,
and they are, too, a "lay," "sweet," pleasur-
able. It was the high, poetic truth that was
first with the ancient Hebrew poet; and it
would seem that poets since have kept truth
first just in proportion as they have approached
the ancient Hebrew poet's power. For what
other reason so much as for this, do Dante,
Shakespeare and Milton hold their places of
lofty isolation? Yes, truth was first with
these, it was first with Wordsworth; and all,

evenly with their bequest of poetic truth, have bequeathed the inevitable, the identical legacy of pleasure, the possession of joy.

As poetry is something different from science and philosophy, something more than these, so we find it something more than history, more than any of the other arts. Cervantes tells us why it is more than history: "The poet may say or sing, not as things were, but as they ought to have been." Here we have a return of the ideal, the true beauty, the far, perfect unity. Be the theme nature, it must be the spirit of nature, the life within and behind, penetrated to, trilled, drilled, to — seen, by the eye of imagination, and found *good;* be the theme man, it is man not in his waywardness, not in his weakness, his despair, but man at his best, in his rightful strength, armed with faith, clothed in joy, transfigured in the undimmed lustre, the gracious radiance poured from the central sun of truth and beauty. Plato, likewise, is simply the voice of the old notion when he says, "Poetry comes nearer than history to the vital truth."

And how stands poetry among the arts? As Fuller finely says, "The arts may be said to be arched together." In this arch of beauty, poetry has a longer curve than painting, than sculpture, than any other of the arts, music excepted. We can trust Lessing on the arch of beauty : —

"If not every trait employed by the descriptive poet can produce an equally good effect on canvas, or in marble, can every trait of the artist be equally effective in the work of the poet ? Undoubtedly, for what pleases us in a work of art pleases not the eye, but the imagination through the eye. The same pictures, whether presented to the imagination by arbitrary or natural signs, must always give us a similar pleasure, though not always in the same degree."

The reference here is to a single phase of the poet's power, the picturing power. Even

under this restriction we shall find that the
sweep of poetry is immeasurably greater than
that of either of the two great picturing arts,
painting and sculpture. The painter puts one
picture on his canvas, the poet presents a
succession of pictures. New visions are con-
tinuously opening, not to distract from the
central picture, but in sympathy with it,
linked with it, circle within circle, to enrich
it to whatsoever extent the imagination may
be able to receive. Landscape painting is
defined by Hamerton as a "mindful interpre-
tation of mind; that is to say, an interpreta-
tion by human genius of the mind that created
the world." Sir Thomas Browne says, "Art
is the perfection of nature. . . . In brief, all
things are artificial, for nature is the art of
God." The office of painting, then, is to re-
produce by one kind of the art of man the art
of God. To see how limited the painter's
art is, compared with the poet's, we have but
to turn from the best landscape painting to a
poet's reproduction of natural scenery : —

" The point of one white star is quivering still
   Deep in the orange light of widening morn,
   Beyond the purple mountains ; through a chasm
   Of wind-divided mist the darker lake
   Reflects it; now it wanes, it gleams again.

.   .   .   .

Beneath is a wide plain of billowy mist,

.   .   .   .

.   Behold it, rolling on
   Under the curdling winds, and islanding
   The peak whereon we stand, midway, around
   Encinctured by the dark and blooming forests,
   Dim twilight lawns, and stream-illumined caves,
   And wind-enchanted shapes of wandering mist ;
   And far on high the keen sky-cleaving mountains
   From icy spires of sunlike radiance fling
   The dawn."

Again, turn from any marine painting to
four lines of Coleridge : —

" Still as a slave before his lord,
   The ocean hath no blast ;
   His great bright eye most silently
   Up to the moon is cast."

Before leaving this part of our inquiry —
if the thoughts be not already too familiar —
let us repeat some of Cousin's sayings on
poetry as one of the fine arts.

" Art," he says, "is the representation of the ideal; this definition gives us a standard by which to compare and classify the fine arts. The first rank should be assigned to the one which, of all others, has the most distinct and intelligible expression, — that is poetry. Next comes music, whose material means, though less determined and distinct than language, produce emotions more profound and vivid than the colors of a painting or the lines of a statue. Painting, sculpture, and architecture are placed last, because their action, more limited, has in view works more special and confined than that of poetry, or of music, and consequently at a greater distance from the ideal."

Cousin has another saying in this connection: " A word, especially a word chosen and transfigured by poetry, is the most energetic and universal symbol."

Poetry comes first because it reaches nearest the ideal, because, music excepted, it has by far the longer curve of the arch of arts. We have also support for our view of the poet's speech: his words are "chosen and transfigured."

Still keeping on the lower level of natural description, note the magic choice, the transfiguration of the common, simple words in Blake's "Evening Star:" —

"Thou fair-haired angel of the evening,
  Now, whilst the sun rests on the mountains, light
  Thy bright torch of love — thy radiant crown
  Put on, and smile upon our evening bed!
  Smile on our loves; and while thou drawest the
  Blue curtains of the sky, scatter thy silver dew
  On every flower that shuts its sweet eyes
  In timely sleep. Let thy west wind sleep on
  The lake ; speak, silence, with thy glimmering eyes,
  And wash the dusk with silver."

We hear too much, be it repeated, concerning originality in poetry; we should hear more of perception, of penetration, of right seeing, of the faithful report.

Those holding the Mill emotional theory, the Macaulay magic-lantern theory, the amuse-

ment, the drawing-room theory, or any other
belittling theory, of poetry, cannot accept its
inevitableness, its accuracy ; but those that
look to poetry as a support, those that lean
upon it, that put their preservation in its safe-
keeping, must receive it as the nearest approach
to truth.   Right seeing is but another word for
accuracy ; truth is but still another word for it.
Coleridge's master, the Rev. James Boyer, gave
him early in life a wholesome lesson on the
accuracy, the logic, of what is commonly
deemed the loose, wayward method of poetry.

"I learned from him," Coleridge says, "that
poetry, even that of the loftiest and seemingly
the wildest odes, had a logic of its own, as
severe as that of science ; and more difficult,
because more subtle, more complex, and depen-
dent on more and more fugitive causes."

The brilliant, ill-starred Buckle says, "The
most accurate investigators of the human mind
have hitherto been the poets."

But the best sayings, the very best, compre-

hensive as they are, after all how fragmentary
in the attempt to exhaust, to fasten the elu-
sive, the limitless, the deathless power of
poetry! As we choose one here and there
among the many that may be readily recalled,
we simply emphasize the futility of the en-
deavor. Horace may say, "If the poet be
silent, you will not receive a reward for your
deeds of glory. . . . The muse forbids the noble
to die"; Bacon may say, "Poetry conferreth
to magnanimity, morality, and to delectation";
Milton may say, "These abilities" [the poet's]
"are the inspired gifts of God, rarely bestowed,
and are of power to imbreed and cherish in a
great people the seeds of virtue and public
civility; to allay the perturbation of the mind,
and set the affections in right tune; and to cel-
ebrate in glorious and lofty hymns the throne
and equipage of God's almightiness"; Voltaire
may say, "Poetry is the music of the soul, and
above all, of great and feeling souls"; Doctor
Johnson may say, The poet " must write as the

interpreter of Nature and the legislator of mankind, and consider himself as presiding over thoughts and manners of future generations, as being superior to time and place "; Goethe may say, " Who twines from unmeaning green leaves a wreath for merits of all kinds? Who insures Olympus, associates gods? Man's lofty spirit revealed in the bard "; Schiller may say, It is the privilege of poetry "to give to humanity its fullest possible expression, its most complete utterance"; Hegel may say, " The proper business of poetry seems to be a representation of the eternal, the ever important and universally beautiful "; Wordsworth may say, " Poetry is the breath and fine spirit of all knowledge, it is the impassioned expression which is in the countenance of all science "; Coleridge may say, " Poetry is the blossom and the fragrancy of all human knowledge, human thoughts, human passions, emotion, language "; Carlyle may say, " The poet penetrates the sacred mystery of the universe — what Goethe calls the ' open secret '

— open to all, seen by almost none "; Emerson may say, The poet is a "sovereign, and stands on the centre. . . the poets are liberating gods "; Thoreau, pressing close to the breast of Nature, may say, " It is only by a miracle that poetry is written at all "; constellation˙ to constellation, the brightest stars of literature may hallow poetry with their united glory; age to age may pay honor to poetry, joy bringing her choicest offerings, and sorrow worshipping silently at its shrine; — still shall we find the reverence unexpressed, the homage poor.

Finally, he is a poet that sees anything, the smallest thing, sufficiently; he is a great poet that sees life sufficiently. Yet this is not all; for out of the seeing must gush the clear, the flowing, the glowing and glorious utterance. " Poetry requires," says Emerson, " that splendor of expression which carries with it the proof of great thoughts." And it must not be forgotten that a still older word for the poet

than the "maker" is the "singer." Nature
says, "I make many half poets, few whole
poets; the hearers are many, the voices few."
We are all partial poets, or the whole poets
would speak in vain; their bright singing
would be dark riddles to us. In our too gra-
cious moods, or because of our ignorance or
our forgetfulness of what poetry is, we some-
times try to patch up partial poets into whole
poets, to make our poets Nature's poets; it is
an empty endeavor. Time, the dispassionate
handmaid of Nature, undoes our work: the
partial poets, the poets that "tell" but do not
"know," the poets that "know" but cannot
"tell," drop away. Only those that "know
and tell," only Nature's own, remain. It is
affirmed that, the thought poetically conceived,
the bright-harnessed angel-words wait in order
serviceable. This is true of the whole poets;
this it is that makes them whole. It is not
true of the partial poets; this it is, in turn,
that makes them partial. .

According to the old notion, poetry is exceedingly difficult; and for the exercise of it, for the summoning forth of the soul of all things, the incarnation of the spirit, the ultimate good, the ever beautiful, in a becoming body, are required the highest faculties of the mind, and the nicest balance of these faculties. In this "whole burst of the mind" are united high seriousness, which never wanders from vital principles, which reveres and holds to the ideal, the very real; experience the deepest and richest; sympathy, quick to respond to the true, the good, the beautiful, and, as a part of this, the meekness Jesus speaks of as the vantage ground of the child; hope, steadfast and triumphant, the trust that refuses any darker saying than *He saw that it was good;* enthusiasm, love, which suffuses with the colors of youth the gray of age and wisdom, which is the flame that plays above the glowing but motionless embers of the intellect; desire, ceaseless, insatiable; severity, severity of thought,

and lastly, that all may not be lost, severity of
speech, the dual severity which admits no
flaw, which is perfection : —

> " For 'tis the eternal law
> That first in beauty should be first in might."

II

WHO ARE THE GREAT POETS?

II

WHO ARE THE GREAT POETS?

IN the course of our inquiry into the old notion of poetry, we found the poet less a comely youth with hair hanging in clustered curls, and large, wild-rolling eyes, than an old man with massive head bowed low, his white locks falling like mist to the ground, his eyes closed. We found him a listener, a worshipper, a reporter, an interpreter, the mouthpiece of the Voice. We found his message, poetry, an immense power, the supreme phenomenon of the human mind; we found it difficult and, of necessity, rare. When we say great poets, we have in mind, perhaps, not more than eight. Homer, Æschylus, Sophocles, Euripides, Virgil, Dante, Shakespeare, Milton — these, at least, the world pronounces

45

great poets; and it is of these in particular that Arnold speaks when he says that we are to look to poetry for our solace and stay.

But are these the greatest poets? Are these distinguished by the highest "seriousness," by the most "powerful and beautiful application of ideas to life"? Is it to these that we should turn first for consolation and strength, for inspiration, for glints of the highest joy?

If we agree with Arnold concerning the importance of letters, and the importance of poetry as the best part of letters; if we further agree with him when he says, "To understand that the language of the Bible is fluid, passing, and literary, not rigid, fixed, and scientific, is the first step toward a right understanding of the Bible"; still concurring when he says, "And as long as the world lasts, all who want to make progress in righteousness will come to Israel for inspiration, as to the people who have the sense for righteousness

most glowing and strongest"; — righteousness
being right-living, and the office of the highest
poetry being to instruct us in this, according
to the laws of poetic beauty and truth, — can
we finally agree with Arnold, can we indeed
find him consistent, when he rests upon the
great eight? The judgment indirectly passed
in his words, "As well imagine a man with a
sense for poetry not cultivating it by the help
of Homer and Shakespeare, as a man with a
sense for conduct not cultivating it by the
help of the Bible," — is this the logical con-
clusion of his splendid stretch of testimony?
If the first step toward a right understanding
of the Bible is to find it literature, is not the
second step to find that the best of biblical
literature is its poetry?

Great minds, in the presence of the inscru-
table, opening on the noblest themes, are
imbued with imagination and emotion; they
rise to poetry, the "music of thought con-
veyed to us in the music of language." Prose

does not serve at those supreme moments when the intellect is pressed to its utmost, when the very feelings rise to thought and the spirit itself may be said to think. The whole being rocks with the rhythm, to the measure, of life, — life which certain philosophers have admirably styled, "moving music." Confucius, tottering about the house, face to face with death, adopts the subtile, all-pervading cadence of poetry, audible in the sea and winds, inaudible but ever present, as Pythagoras feigned — or said most truly — in the singing realms of space: —

> " The great mountain is broken,
> The strong beam is thrown down,
> The wise man has decayed."

The ancient Hebrew's appeal from the seen to the Unseen, from the low to the Most High, could not be made without eloquence; in its most impassioned, its surest, its highest form, it could not be made save in the golden cadence of song. Here belongs a saying of Hegel : —

"This superiority, this impressiveness of the Infinite, the immeasurable distance which separates it from the finite — this is what the art of the sublime should express. It is the religious art, the sacred art *par excellence;* its sole destination is to celebrate the glory of God. This office alone poetry can fulfil."

. . . "For to the glory of God and the singing of his glories, no man dares deny, man was chiefly made," says old George Chapman; "and what art performs this chief end of man with so much excitation and expression as poesy, — Moses, David, Solomon, Job, Esay, Jeremy, chiefly using that to the end above said?"

It were hard to say where we may find the most exalted exhibition of the right seeing of life, if not in that half of the Old Testament where the great round, bright words roll augustly through the highest heavens of imagination.

In the sayings just quoted, we again find

poetry and religion one, again find poetry resting on God. Poetry rests on God; there the ancient Hebrews rested as no other people have. Poetry reposes on eternal life; there the Hebrews reposed as no other people have; and in their seeing of life we have a right to expect the highest poetry. We have a right to expect this. Are we disappointed? Arnold says: "If we are said to underrate, for instance, the production of Corneille and Racine in poetry, we may compare this production in power, in penetrativeness, in criticism of life, in ability to call forth our energy and joy, with the production of Homer and Shakespeare." May we not so say of Homer and Shakespeare, in comparison with Isaiah and the author of Job? Again, speaking of the student of poetry, Arnold says: —

"As he penetrates into the spirit of the great classical works, as he becomes gradually aware of their intense significance, their noble simplicity, and their calm pathos, he will be

convinced that it is this effect, unity and
profoundness of moral impression, at which
the ancient poets aimed; that it is this which
constitutes the grandeur of their works, and
which makes them immortal."

May we not say that all this, applicable
enough to the poets of Greece, to which it
mainly refers, is still more applicable to the
poets of the ancient Hebrews? Why, then,
was Arnold wont to rest upon the poetry of
Greece? Surely not because the substance of
the Greek poetry is to be put before the sub-
stance of the Hebrew poetry. If not the
substance, then it is the form that deterred
him from following his own theories to what
would seem to be their legitimate · result.
Were the forms of the Hebrew poetry less
inevitably the result of the Hebrew substance,
we should still claim that the greater value of
the Hebrew substance would more than com-
pensate for the loss in form; but is there a
loss in form?

Let us first make sure that it was the intent of the Hebrew poet to write poetry. Friedrich Bleek, in his "Introduction to the Old Testament," says : —

"The distinction between the poetical and prose style of composition is the one that can be perceived the most decidedly and certainly. The poetic style of the Hebrews is not distinguished from the prose by any prescribed metre, but by a certain rhythmical measurement and division of the periods and separate sentences, and also by many linguistic peculiarities, the form of words, grammatical constructions and inflections, which are not used in the prose." Again, he says, "This distinction between prose composition and that which is allowable in poetry, prevails in all languages ; but in no other language whatever do we find the expressions which are unusual in prose, and allowable solely in poetical composition, stamped so distinctly as they are in Hebrew."

So it was by direct intention that the He-
brew poet wrote as a poet. Now as to the
forms he used: "But in the poetry of the
Hebrew, besides this aphoristic biblical form,
there is another peculiar law of living, breath-
ing thought and rhythmical motion, not in-
deed of words and syllables, but of images
and feelings, undulating in free symmetry like
the waves of the sea."

Schlegel's idea of the rhythm of thought
is both beautiful and true; but though we
can know nothing of the quantity that entered
into the construction of Hebrew verse, are we
not warranted in inferring that, in addition
to the rhythm of thought, or of "senti-
ment," as another terms it, it had a rhythmi-
cal motion of words and syllables? The
ancient Hebrew poetry was not in Greek verse,
but can we say that it "was not in verse"?
Mr. Theodore Watts speaks singularly well
on the point of rhythm: "Perhaps it may be
said that deeper than all the rhythms of art

is that rhythm which art would fain catch, the rhythm of nature; for the rhythm of nature is the rhythm of life itself. This rhythm can be caught by prose as well as by poetry, such prose, for instance, as that of the English Bible. Certainly the rhythm of verse at its highest, such, for instance, as that of Shakespeare's greatest writings, is nothing more and nothing less than the metre of that energy of the spirit which surges within the bosom of him who speaks, whether he speak in verse or impassioned prose. Being rhythm, it is of course governed by law, but it is a law which transcends in subtlety the conscious art of the metricist, and is only caught by the poet in his most inspired moods; a law which, being part of nature's own sanctions, can of course never be formulated, but only expressed as it is expressed in the melody of the bird, in the inscrutable harmony of the entire bird-chorus of a thicket, in the whisper of the leaves of the tree, and the song or wail of wind and sea."

In this admirable passage the ancient Hebrew poet, though read in translation, is paired with our great dramatist: both have a "rhythm deeper than all the rhythms of art." Had Arnold meant this when he said the Hebrews were without art, we should find, as we cannot now, the last link in his chain of perceptions and reasonings of the pure metal of those that lead to it. One may say, if one choose, that the Hebrew poets had something higher than art; we are content to say that they had art, — art as adequate for the expression of their poetry as the art of the Greeks for the expression of theirs. We say further that, their subject-matter being incomparably higher, their seeing of life wider and deeper by far, than that of the Greek poets, their art was correspondingly higher; it was the virgin gold worked into shapes beyond the cunning of even the Grecian hand, the inevitable shapes of the high, hidden might of the elemental powers. We say that their thoughts have a beautiful, sympathetic body, in which they live and will ever live. "*L'art est une forme*": such is the form of the greatest art.

The theme of Homer is the "Anger of Achilles." Around this revolves all his masterly array of human action in a world practically without the pale of the one of all the powers indispensable to the great critic of life — moral law. It is not till after Homer's day that we arrive at this law; and how weak, how dim and wavering, it is even in Euripides, compared with the Hebrew poet! "Poetic beauty and poetic truth" Homer most assuredly has; but we cannot look to him for the most powerful and beautiful criticism of life. Homer's theme is the "Anger of Achilles," the Hebrew poet's theme is, —

"The Eternal loveth the thing that is right."

It is true indeed that righteousness came into Greek poetry; it is equally true that it went

out again. It is equally true, also, that it
came into Hebrew poetry and stayed in it.
The Hebrew lyre was tuned to righteousness
from first to last. In the serious days of
northern Greece, in the great successors of
Homer, are to be found high criticisms of life,
but none comparable with the criticisms of
those who invariably give as a reason for
being of their song, —

     "His word was in my tongue."

Great poetry, as we have said, rests on God,
and the great poetry is to be looked for on the
old ground, on Arnold's ground, among the
Hebrew poets; they, and they alone, were, as
Fox says of Tyndale, "practised in God's mat-
ters." The Hebrew poet's higher, wider out-
look on life is evidenced by his God. The
Greek poet had gods that he could adequately
express; of the Hebrew poet's God no words
could give the faintest outline. The expres-
sions of the worshippers of Zeus and of
Jehovah must differ; but to say that one has

all the art, not only denies the cardinal principle that noble conception has for its handmaid noble expression, but reduces form to an inflexible, fixed thing. Form is pliant, it follows the life. Nature has infinite forces of life and infinite forms; and it would seem that in proportion as poets — not to consider other artists — near the marvellous variety of nature, the more do they vary from a fixed form of expression. The Hebrew poets and Shakespeare employ varieties of expression that, with the Greek poetry as a standard, appear decidedly irregular; but let us beware lest deceived by a surface irregularity, we fail to see beneath a deeper, a more subtile regularity, an order closer to the order of the "art of God."

Whitman has a noteworthy saying in this connection. " Poetic style," he says, " when addressed to the soul is less definite form, outline, sculpture, and becomes vista, music, half-tints, and even less than half-tints."

These words are spoken in defence of a

certain obscurity; but if we stop with the word "music," they are of equal or greater value as a defence of the freedom of structure characterizing the ancient Hebrew poetry. Let us not forget that poetry is one thing and sculpture another. Let us not be too sure that the art of the Hebrew poets and of Shakespeare is inferior to the art of the Greek poets; that beneath the apparent disobedience to rule is not a deeper obedience, which deeper obedience springs of a lower, a harder, hold on life. We think it indisputable that the Hebrew poets had a firmer hold on life than the Greek poets had; hence that it is to the Hebrew poets that we are to turn first for solace, for support, for "self-preservation"

"Against the wreckful siege of battering days."

While by no means denying that in the poetry of the Old Testament, as in other great poetry, there is much that is not poetry, we affirm that the under-current of great song is there, unfailing, and stronger than it is elsewhere to be found.

From one point of view we do the Greek poets injustice by comparing them with the Hebrew poets through the medium of translation; for not only does the Hebrew expression lend itself more readily to translation, but rarely may we meet with such prodigies of reproduction as the chief translators of the English Bible. An eminent critic says of Tyndale, "He felt, by a happy instinct, the potential affinity between Hebrew and English idioms." This observation, besides honoring Tyndale's genius, points to one of the sources of the Hebrew poet's advantage over the Greek poet when read in our own language. From another point of view, the use of translations is just; for it discloses a most important fact, viz., that, allowance being made for inferior translation, the ancient Hebrew poetry is the only pure poetry, the only poetry that is poetry through and through, the only poetry that holds its virtue against the sapping accents of a stranger-tongue. This fact of itself would seem to be sufficient to warrant the statement that the highest poetry is to be found, not in the adorable Homer, magnificent witness that he was to the truths of nature and of man, but in the Book of Job; that the Hebrew muse

" Filled Isaiah's breast with more than Pindar's fire."

While admitting the gain of the Hebrew poets over the Greek in translation, it is but right to note one of the many serious disadvantages to the Hebrew poets, that of a wretchedly scrappy arrangement. Probably it would be difficult to exaggerate the havoc that has been made in the continuity of the original Hebrew. We have fragments of the sacred song of the Hebrews, mutilated and patched as it has survived the not very tender mercy of centuries; while of their secular song barely enough remains to suggest what it was.

" For an enduring heart have the destinies appointed to
the children of men."

Arnold, in his earnest, lucid and beautiful
manner, has testified to the excellence of this
Homeric expression. But for substance, for
form, for any of the attributes of poetry,
wherein is it to be put before

"For he
That feareth God shall come forth of them all,"
or before

" Great peace have they which love thy law,"
or before

" Be still, and know that I am God " ?

And where in Æschylus or in Sophocles, in
Dante or in Milton, shall we find an equal
number of lines the perfect form of which does
not shrink and shrivel in the presence of that
most august song that has ever fallen from the
lips of man, the 90th Psalm ?   Recall the clos-
ing words, the words of all words for the sup-
plication of the sovereign poet : —

" Let the beauty of the Lord our God be upon us."

And where, forsooth, may we look in the classics for solace, for defence against the wreckful siege, such as is to be found in the 23d Psalm?

> "He leadeth me beside the still waters,
> He restoreth my soul."

We look in vain among the Greek poets for this reach.   And if we seek a God, where shall we find another like the Unutterable One grasped at with the last stretch of sublimity in Job XXVI: 5–11?   And where but in poets with such a God shall we find a criticism of life in any way comparable to this?

> "Man that is born of woman is of few days,
>   And full of trouble.
> He cometh forth like a flower,
>   And is cut down;
> He fleeth also as a shadow and continueth not.
>   .   .   .   .
> And surely the mountain falling cometh to naught,
> And the rock is removed out of his place.
> The waters wear the stones :
> Thou washest away the things which grow out of the dust
>   of the earth;
> And thou destroyest the hope of man.
> Thou prevailest forever against him and he passeth:
> Thou changest his countenance and sendest him away."

No volumes in our knowledge give so nearly complete a history of man as is written here. All, all is compassed in the last eight words; words, to use the expression of Job, which do indeed break us in pieces. But hark! again the old sweet words return, the words glowing forever in the Hebrew poet's soul, burning on steadfastly, brightly, behind the darkness: —

> "Why art thou cast down, O my Soul?
> And why art thou disquieted within me?
> Hope thou in God."

The Hebrew poet's soul breathes a hope which to the Greek poet was impossible: —

> "My flesh also shall rest in hope,
> .   .   .   .   .   .
> Yet in my flesh shall I see God."

"The best that has been thought and said in the world" has for its basis unshaken faith, glorious hope; and we have a larger utterance of this than "the large utterance of the early gods." In short, the Hebrew poet stands for conduct not only, but for high right-seeing, for

the nearest perfect expression of the mother-
life, the mother-music, in which we move.

> " For though the giant ages heave the hill,
>   And break the shore, and evermore
>   Make and break and work their will;
>   Though world on world in myriad myriads roll,
>   Round us, each with different powers
>   And other forms of life than ours,
>   What know we greater than the soul ?
>   On God and god-like men we build our trust."

Only this trust, held in the measure that the
Hebrew poet held it, can help us to discern the
" hieroglyphic meanings of human suffering,"
can lead us in the way of patience, can inspire
us, despite perplexity and sorrow and darkness,
with the light, the certainty, the joy, which the
poet finds the right to say shall be.

The recognized tendency of the poet to open
the heart of the things we say we know, and to
display them in the mother-light of beauty,
leads to a final reach toward what we say we do
not know, but hope for — the things that high-
est intuitions and widest experience say should
be ; and this last reach, this golden guess, is

poetry's consummation. Poetry, in the exercise of its highest function, takes up this world, this life, where it breaks, crumbles under us ; takes it up, and rounds all once more into symmetry, pressing on unsatisfied to voice the spirit's prophecy of the perfecting world, the perfecting life, beyond. The ancient Hebrew poets addressed themselves to this ultimate revelation ; and it is by their success here that they stand apart from all other poets of whatever time or race, the glory and the wonder of the world.

After the addition of Roman stoicism, yes, after the incomparably greater addition of Christianity, we can still learn from the Greek poets, can still profit by study of them. We of to-day can get a great deal from the song of old Greece, but not this last revelation. The stamp of manliness, the rigorous will, the blissful indifference, the pleasant taking of what comes, the patient questioning of nature, and the faith in it, the blessing of health, the beauty of beauties — the beauty of youth, openness,

clearness, freedom of mind, the best methods
of intelligence, — for all of these (and our need
of them is sore) we can go back and sit with
attentive Athens in the temple of Bacchus.
But when the lustre of youth and beauty grows
dim in our souls, as it grew dim in the soul of
Greece and departed from it; when the dark
problems lower, when the gray mist, gathered
of the ages, drifts in ; when the viewless bur-
den is fully on our shoulders, and we cannot
stand, — then we must turn, not to the poets
that avoided with so amazing grace the dark-
ness, the drift, and the weight, but to the poets
that met these face to face, met them, bore up
under them, conquered, leaving to the world
the imperishable heritage of hope.

While it is evident that the first aim of the
Hebrew poet is not the artist's aim, it seems
equally plain that no other poet has more faith-
fully obeyed the great underlying laws of
poetic construction. He may weave the finest
net-work of artificiality, as in that standing mar-

vel of composition for all ages, the Book of Job; he may give a brilliant exhibition of metrical technics, as in Lamentations and in Psalm 119; but it is in the use, the choice, of words — and there is the vital place — that we find him without a peer. If we may credit Professor W. Robertson Smith, the very structure of his language forced the Hebrew into poetry : —

. . . "The key to the whole development of the poetical literature of Israel is found in the same psychological characteristics of the race which are impressed on the vocabulary and grammatical structure of the language. The Hebrew tongue is sensuous, mobile, passionate."

Here we have in the language itself the essentials of poetry as set down by Milton. The Hebrew poet's very language, preventing him from metaphysics, made and kept him a poet. Professor Smith goes on : —

"Unfit for abstract speculation, valuing no wisdom that is not practical, and treasuring up

such wisdom in sententious rhythmical form,
enforced by symbol and metaphor, and warm
with the breath of human interest, — the
Hebrew is a poet, even in his philosophy."

If individual poets are born, why not nations
of poets? A race of poets — so we may name
the old Hebrews.

Professor Smith has described the genius of
the Hebrew tongue; now let Dr. Curtius per-
form a like office for the Greek tongue.

"Far above all its sister tongues," says Dr.
Curtius, "the Greek must be regarded as a
work of art, on account of the sense prevalent
in it for symmetry and perfection of sounds, for
transparency of form, for law and organization.
. . . The Hellenes must have received the
material of language while it was yet a plastic
form; otherwise, they could never have suc-
ceeded in expressing, by means of it, as in the
most ductile clay, the whole variety of their
spiritual gifts, their artistic sense of form, as
well as *that severity of abstract thought which,*

long before it manifested itself in the books of their philosophers, was already apparent in the grammar of their language."

The lines italicized are rich in significance. The philosopher, both in substance and method, lies in embryo by the side of the poet in the grammar of the Greek language; while the Hebrew grammar gives no sign of any other than the poet. The Hebrew had but to speak to be a poet : —

" Mine enemy sharpeneth his eyes upon me."

.   .   .   .

" The waters are hid as with a stone."

.   .   .   .

" The moon walking in brightness."

.   .   .   .

" Dost thou know the balancings of the clouds ? "

The poets of Greece reflect nature beautifully, but if we are to see the very expression of her countenance, if we are to feel her warm breath, the throbbing of her heart, we must turn to the poets of Palestine.

" As when about the silver moon, when air is free from wind,
  And stars shine clear to whose sweet beams, high prospects,
      and the brows
  Of all steep hills and pinnacles, thrust up themselves for
    shows,
  And even the lovely valleys joy to glitter in their sight,
  When the unmeasured firmament bursts to disclose her
    light,
  And all the sights in heaven seen that glad the shepherd's
    heart," etc.

These lines of Homer have been greatly admired, and it would be strange indeed had they not been; but the intense sympathy with nature, the brooding pathos, is left for the hand that wrote, —

  " He *quieteth* the earth by the south wind."

When the Hebrew poet makes use of nature, it is the gentle voice of the mother herself : —

" Knowest thou the time when the wild goats of the rock
    bring forth ?
  Or canst thou mark when the hinds do calve ?
  Canst thou number the mouths that they fulfil ?
  Or knowest thou the time when they bring forth ?
  They bow themselves, they bring forth their young ones,
  They cast out their sorrows."

Hegel may call Homer the " Master-poet of

living Nature," but after reading these lines,
one must say that if Hegel speak truly, Nature,
through the sons of another than the Greek
race, hushed the human voice, and spoke with
her own.

If we pass from tenderness and pathos to the
mutterings of the thunder that interrupted
Elihu; if we pass through the terrible storm
that rages still on the sacred page as it did in
the ears of Job and his counsellors; if we pass
to the voice of the God of the thunder, we are
ushered into the presence of sublimity of con-
ception and expression reached only by the
people that, whatever their short-comings may
be, have a right, because of their unapproachable
poetry, to the name of the People of God.

Froude's words concerning the book of Job
have the right ring: —

. . . "A book of which it is to say little to
call it unequalled of its kind, and which will
one day, perhaps, when it is allowed to stand
on its own merits, be seen towering up

alone, far away above all the poetry of the world."

The question is not, Did the author of Job follow the rules of the epic as laid down by Aristotle? The question is not, Does Bishop Cox speak accurately when he says, " Hebrew poetry consists of every possible species of poetical composition, and these are all carried to the loftiest pitch of excellence ? " The question is, If the Hebrew poets did not have what Arnold would have us understand by "the inexplicable form and texture that is eternal," did they not really have it? The question is, Whatever they had not, did they not have before all other poets, the ability to criticise life, to criticise it according to the laws of poetic beauty and poetic truth ; did they not have the strength, the splendid strength upon which the world has leaned, now leans, and will continue to lean, hardest for its support and stay?

Arnold could find in Wordsworth a substi-

tute for style: " inevitableness," " expression
of the most truly expressive kind." We can-
not account for his failure to find this, if not
style, in the poetry of the ancient Hebrews.
We cannot find him consistent with himself in
turning first and last to the classics. Tyndale,
speaking of his early days at Oxford and Cam-
bridge, says, " In the universities they have
ordained that no man shall look at the Scrip-
tures until he be noselled [nursed] in heathen
learning eight or nine years." In the matter of
poetry are we not being noselled too long?

III

MATTHEW ARNOLD

III

MATTHEW ARNOLD

"* * * virtues like these
Make human nature shine, reform the soul,
And break our fierce barbarians into men."

Cato i. 4: ADDISON.

COULD Matthew Arnold rise from his still place and be induced to read the reviews of his work published since he passed from sight, he would find one declaring him primarily a poet, another, essentially a critic. He would learn that, as a critic, he is to be trusted, now, for his knowledge and insight, again, to be read principally for the personal flavor which makes appetizing biased, not to say eccentric, judgments; he would discover that the sharp contradictions concerning him cease only in the agreement that his voice, whether with cadence of verse or of prose, is the voice of doubt. Since Arnold was incapable of ambiguous expression, the responsibility for this difference of opinion is fixed upon his readers; unless, indeed, his writings be, like those of the reviewers, a mass of self-contradiction. As to self-contradiction, it will hardly be denied that generally Arnold was only less consistent than clear; hence the clashing of the reviewers must be attributed to lack of serious intent, of close, respectful attention, of fulness of thought, of sobriety of temper, of mellowness of judgment, — to the absence of qualities that this lost leader along the upper paths was wont to include in the now so familiar word, culture.

Arnold declared his purpose to be a "disinterested endeavor to learn and propagate the best that is known and thought in the world." This is to take a high stand, and an inquiry into his achievements should be conducted with high-mindedness. The aim should be to get at the heart of his life-labor, to lay hold on the best of it; passing belittling questions as to

whether he, at times, walked among us with an
iron spine, or occasionally paused to put his
finger on some minor blemish, and, by over-
nicety, magnify it to a plague spot.   Three of
Arnold's round dozen volumes are poetry.   The
relative bulk of these two kinds of writing is
noteworthy; for where one's gift is, there, as a
rule, will it be exercised.   Four times as many
volumes of prose as of verse indicates that the
writer's thought rides easiest in the vehicle of
prose.   Indeed, Arnold has stated that he be-
lieved his essays to be his most important work,
especially the essays devoted to religion.   It is
difficult to form a contrary opinion unless upon
the ground before stated, — the failure to bring
to an examination of his writings a right mind
and temper.

   It is said that, because Arnold began writing
in verse, verse is his natural voice.   Verse is
the first voice of us all, of nations as well as of
individuals; for it is the voice of youth.   It is
the *lumen purpureum juventae*, glowing on into

age, that tunes gray years to the measure of song. The young writer of emphatically a poetic temperament begins as a singer; and it is the test of time that shows him and the world whether he is a poet, or merely a person poetically disposed. But if Arnold was not primarily a poet, his bent toward poetry was so strong, and his capacity for culture so rare, that, all but in the face of elemental law, he climbed to an enviable height the very Helicon. He did not storm the outer gates of song, but by most subtile ingenuity arrayed himself in the shining robe of the elect, deceived them, and passed quietly in as one of themselves. He knew what poetry is, his faculties were obedient, his sympathies irresistible; art mothered him after the wont of nature, that he might match himself against the born son of the muse. Insight, appreciation, patience — these are the qualities that stamp the born critic; and so intrinsically was Arnold a critic, that he seized not only the livery but the secret of the creators, and advanced himself far along their own lines. His was an unchallenged entry into the outer gates of song; it was only within the golden circle of the lyrists that he could not come. There is a limit to the victory of culture; much of Arnold's poetry is but thrice-refined criticism, trebly refined pessimistic criticism; and the portion of it that is pure poetry is not song. The born critic could not learn the born poet's lay; but he could rise to noble verse, indeed to as noble verse of the kind as we have in the language. Stedman has pointed to the fact that Arnold "almost falsified the adage that a poet is born"; the point here made is, that valuable as " Sorab and Rustum," " Thyrsis," and the "Scholar-Gypsy " are as poetry, they are of still greater value as testimony to the exceedingly rare gifts that made the author the first critic of our time; the first critic, not literary nor religious nor social critic merely, but the first critic foursquare, — fitted to see the complex mystery called life as nearly as it is as lies to-day in man's ability.

Arnold's poems inspired by the Greek spirit are drawn fresh from the font; and if he is less successful in the region of romance, ample amends are made when we find that he has but two peers among us in narrative verse. All his metrical writing is welcomed by the cultured mind, and more stress would now be put on his bequest of verse were it not that, good and valuable as it is, his prose is of still greater worth. Didacticism and pessimism constitute the main objection to the body of his poetry, — too naked teaching, too free use of the "fearful gift," the "glance of melancholy," too much malady and too little melody, too little ease and spontaneity, too little of the bubbling music of joy which the masters have taught us to demand. Yes, there is too much of the tutor, of the "immedicable soul," and too little of the happy pipe-player; finally, too much of Etna and elsewhere, and too little home matter; but the gentle, self-centred spirit is ever present, and, as a rule, the cunning of art. Philosophy

proper, plodding philosophy, and poesy get
along together no better than youth and age;
still, it would be an ungrateful world that could
feel no sense of indebtedness for such lines as
the following from a poem once withdrawn,
afterward put forth with misgivings: —

" Is it so small a thing
    To have enjoyed the sun,
  To have lived light in the spring,
    To have loved, to have thought, to have done ;
  To have advanced true friends, and beat down baffling
      foes ?

I say: Fear not! Life still
    Leaves human effort scope.
  But, since life teems with ill,
    Nurse no extravagant hope ;
  Because thou must not dream, thou needst not then
      despair."

But if Arnold does not greatly impress us as
a poet, the moment we meet him as a critic we
are in the presence of a master. Let not the
delicacy of touch deceive us as to the thorough-
ness of the work, fatal to confusion of the true
and the false as is the whirlwind of right-

eous wrath. The preface to "Literature and Dogma" and that to Wordsworth's poems — these two short essays of themselves proclaim Arnold the keenest, the wisest critic so far adorning English literature. The corner-stone of his critical building is culture, the definition of which — made with special reference to Biblical criticism, but serving equally well elsewhere — is "the acquainting ourselves with the best that has been known and said in the world, and thus with the history of the human spirit; which turns out to be, in another shape, and, in particular relation to the Bible, — getting the power, through reading, to estimate the proportion and relation in what we read." "If we read but a very little," he continues, "we naturally want to press it all; if we read a great deal, we are willing not to press the whole of what we read, and we learn what ought to be pressed and what not. Now this is really the very foundation of any sane criticism."

Nor yet is this severe preparation sufficient;

there remains the gift unattainable, and so rarely inborn, without which erudition, conscience, patience, must fall short: —

"After we have acquainted ourselves with the best that has been known in the world, after we have got all the facts of our special study, fineness and delicacy of perception to deal with the facts is still required, and is, even, the principal thing of all."

For one that shot his beams over the broad field of life, it was easy to cover the centre of the field, the flower-patch of literature, with a flood of white light. Whether he considers the Rev. Mr. Brooke's "Primer," or Macaulay's estimate of Milton, or rises to the majestic heights of Milton himself, the qualifications that he has declared indispensable to his office are manifest, and are employed with the same care, the same temperate effectiveness. The four cardinal virtues of a primer of English literature are declared to be " clearness, brevity, proportion, sobriety." A truth apparent enough; ay, but this and many another self-evident truth were left for Arnold to fix in imperishable utterance. A single sentence etches Macaulay's strength and weakness: " A style brilliant, metallic, exterior, making strong points, alternating invective with eulogy, wrapping in a robe of rhetoric the thing it presents; not, with the soft play of life, following and rendering the thing's very form and pressure."

The memorable summing up of Milton's powers — memorable not only because of its masterliness, but as the last word to us of this authentic voice — stands, a pyramid, on the waste of every-day criticism : —

" That Milton, of all our English race, is by his diction and rhythm the one artist of the highest rank in the great style whom we have; this I take as requiring no discussion, this I take as certain. The mighty power of poetry and art is generally admitted. But where the soul of this power, of this power at its best,

chiefly resides, very many of us fail to see. It
resides chiefly in the refining and elevation
wrought in us by the high and rare excellence
of the great style. . . . Milton has made the
great style no longer an exotic here; he has
made it an inmate amongst us, a leaven, and
a power."

If this exaltation of the critical spirit and
power is familiar now, the high voice so
recently silenced has made it so. "There was
no literary critic in England," says the veteran
Stoddard, "before Matthew Arnold."

The essentials of just criticism, admirably
registered in the preface to "Literature and
Dogma," are as admirably exemplified in the
preface to Wordsworth's poems, the impor-
tance of poetry and the seriousness of the
critic's task being restated with the accustomed
precision and incision: —

"Now poetry is nothing less than the most
perfect speech of man, that in which he comes
nearest to being able to utter the truth. It is

no small thing, therefore, to succeed eminently in poetry. And so much is required for duly estimating success here that about poetry it is, perhaps, hardest to arrive at a sure general verdict, and takes longest."

Arnold's definition of poetry, as a "criticism of life," has been disparaged by writers from whom were to be hoped better things. The reviewers, not excepting the master spirit of "The Athenæum," seem to follow him but half-way. To say that poetry is at bottom a "criticism of life," is a materially different thing from saying that it is wholly and directly a criticism of life. The context of the phrase must be considered in order to get the meaning: "The greatness of a poet lies in his powerful *and beautiful* application of ideas to life." That is, the great poet must have profound, practical ideas on man and nature, and must express them "under the conditions immutably fixed by the laws of poetic beauty and poetic truth."

Content to leave the definition of poetry —

new only in its phraseology — to its own
defence, let us see with what result the test is
applied to the poems of Wordsworth. Were
Arnold three-fourths Greek, seven-eighths form,
as many make him, Wordsworth would be one
of the first poets to repel him; for, in the
words of the critic himself, "he has no
style." Plainly enough there must be a substi-
tute for style. What has Wordsworth in its
imperial place? He has "expression of the
highest and most truly expressive kind."
With a well-nigh faultless hand, the poet's
shortcomings are weighed against his noble
powers, till we come to the conclusion, equally
remarkable for accuracy and courage,—"I firmly
believe that the poetical performance of Words-
worth is, after that of Shakspeare and Milton
. . . undoubtedly the most considerable in our
language from the Elizabethan age to the
present time."

This is a cry in the wilds, but there is little
risk in asserting, even at this early day, that

the judgment is final. "Wordsworth has an insight into permanent sources of joy." With an article inserted, we have a volume in this supplement of ten words, — "Wordsworth has an insight into *the* permanent sources of joy." A second supplement is to be found in the "Memorial Verses," written some forty years ago : —

> "He found us when the age had bound
> Our souls in its benumbing round;
> He spoke, and loosed our heart in tears.
> He laid us as we lay at birth
> On the cool flowery lap of earth,
> Smiles broke from us and we had ease;
> The hills were round us, and the breeze
> Went o'er the sunlit fields again;
> Our foreheads felt the wind and rain.
> Our youth returned; for there was shed
> On spirits that had long been dead,
> Spirits dried up and closely furl'd,
> The freshness of the early world."

If Arnold's estimate of Wordsworth be just —and who will gainsay it?—, we owe him a debt smaller only than that due the poet himself. It required a mind open as the poet's own, a spirit as responsive to the rhythmic beat of universal life, to see and know him as he is; it required the ability that distinguishes Matthew Arnold as a critic. The essay on Wordsworth has been chosen as an example of Arnold's critical ability, not simply because it is regarded as adequate, just, but because the subject is one that calls for a full showing of the fundamental principles of criticism as he understands them.

Arnold's estimate of Shelley's poetry has not proved generally acceptable. What, in a word, is the estimate? The star-like light of spirit, the floating, evanescent beauty, the exuberant music — these remain, unchallenged; but, with greatness as the standard, a detracting charge is made — the charge of unsubstantiality. The subjects treated are declared to be not of the highest importance : —

" Those who extol him as the poet of clouds, the poet of sunsets, are only saying that he did not, in fact, lay hold upon the poet's — the great poet's — right subject matter; and in honest truth, with all his charm of soul and spirit, with all his charm of musical diction and movement, he never, or hardly ever, did."

The excellencies of Shelley, if not insisted on, are here plainly set down, while what is conceived to be the main deficiency is brought into prominence: his subjects are so remotely related to the life of man that his work is necessarily lacking in human interest, compared, for example, with Wordsworth's, and therefore less effective for the higher purpose of art, which is to reflect, to purify, to enlarge, to ennoble the life of man, to encourage and sustain him in his best efforts to attain fulness of being.—Arnold well knew that this exalted purpose was not to be directly, baldly asserted. He did not mean that the poet should preach (though Wordsworth often fell to it, and he himself has not suffered his master to make the descent alone), but that the preacher's wisdom and earnestness should be behind the utterance, which, for its part, must mask and manage the plain purpose according to the requirements of art. — The standard of judgment, let us not forget, is high, no lower than elementary law ; and tried by it, Shelley stands in shadow. Not to go beyond the shorter poems, the inimitable " Lines to an Indian Air," compared with those of the " Highland Reaper," are less vital and abiding. Let the student of poetry supplement what Arnold says of Shelley's song with the Rev. Stopford Brooke's essay, " Some Thoughts on Shelley," and he cannot get far out of the way. If Arnold has fallen short in the case of Shelley, he has shown us again and again how to find the weak place ; and he has more than once admonished us, when the weak place is found, to leave it and pass on to the next place that is strong.   .

Two articles on Arnold by an American writer, with a charm of his own, have come under our notice. They invite to particular attention because one of them, a review of Arnold's lecture on Emerson, voices a represen-

tative sentiment on this side of the Atlantic;
and the other, a general survey of Arnold's
work, seems to us, excellent as it is in many
respects, to illustrate the tendency among his
critics to follow him only half-way. What
does Arnold say of Emerson? In the rough,
he says that "his observation of nature is
always marvellously fine"; that, while his
"insight is admirable," his "truth precious,"
the secret of his effect is, after all, "in his
hopeful, serene, beautiful temper"; that never
before had man such a sense of the inex-
haustibleness of nature, and such hope; that
for his (Arnold's) ear the early utterances of
Emerson "brought a strain as new, and mov-
ing, and unforgetable, as the strain of . . .
Goethe"; that Emerson's work is the most
important prose work of the century. Surely
this is a rich testimonial, and in it Arnold
shows again that, with all his insistence on
style, on the commanding forms of art, that
there are other things of .greater value. The

lecture reveals no lack of admiration, of love;
and surely it does not detract from Arnold's
matchless equipment for criticism that he can
put his heart aside and speak with the passion-
less accent of the years to come. Emerson has
not the "inestimable virtue of concreteness," he
is constrained to say: " he is not a *great* poet,
nor is he a *great* man of letters, because he
could not subdue his material to the readily
felt but inexplicable form and texture that is
eternal." Though the great poet, yes, the
great man of letters, be taken away, we have
left the great teacher, the great man, the great
isolated Emerson.

In the other paper, the one on Arnold's work
in general, it is stated that he "lays the em-
phasis upon the more select, the high-bred
qualities." While Arnold is constant to these
qualities, if we read him aright he lays the
emphasis on a no higher-bred quality than
right conduct, — plain, simple, well-doing.
" We have seen," he says, " what an immense

matter conduct is; that it is three-fourths of
life. We have seen how plain and simple a
matter it is, so far as knowledge is concerned."
To the extent that Hellenism helps " to get rid
of one's ignorance, to see things as they are,
and by seeing them as they are, to see them in
their beauty " — to this extent do we find him
a Hellene, which is a very different thing from
finding him an embodiment of "pure Hellen-
ism." Hellenism with him stands for intellec-
tual power, Hebraism for moral power, and,
prone as he is to the intelligential side, we have
never failed to find him first and last on the
moral side, a fixture there. Whatever is added,
the foundation is morals: "In praising cul-
ture, we have never denied that conduct, not
culture, is three-fourths of human life." For
all the cry of Greek, we find Arnold less Greek
than Hebrew. In "Literature and Dogma,"
the work he set most by, while the method of
interpreting the Scriptures is Hellenic, the pur-
pose is unmistakably Hebraic, — one steady

testimony to the enduring pith and marrow of
the Bible. The work breathes throughout the
true Hebrew spirit at its highest: "*If ye know
these things, happy are ye if ye do them!* — the
last word for infirm humanity." But Arnold
is neither pure Greek nor pure Hebrew; rather
a blending of the two, a student of the law of
human development. He is a disciple of cul-
ture, by which he means in the large, not "pure
Hellenism," but Hebraism plus Hellenism.
"All the love of our neighbor," are his words,
"the impulses towards action, help, and benefi-
cence, the desire for removing human error,
clearing human confusion, and diminishing
human misery, the noble aspiration to leave
the world better and happier than we found
it, — motives eminently such as are called
social, — come in as part of the grounds of cul-
ture, and the main and pre-eminent part."
"Hebraism, Hellenism," he says, "are neither
of them the *law* of human development; they
are, each of them, contributions to human

development." They are not the law, nor indeed do they seem the sum, the ultimate to which Arnold is ever pointing.

Further on we find this statement: "Another form which Arnold's Hellenism takes is, that it begets in him what we may call the spirit of institutionalism, as opposed to the spirit of individualism. . . . He always takes up for the state against the individual, and for public and established forms against private and personal dissent and caprice."

Were it not for the last word, "caprice," Arnold's position with regard to the individual could hardly be wrested from this statement of it. Arnold *is* against individual caprice, — against individual ignorance, against the individual at his lowest; which is a different thing from being opposed to individual steadfastness and wisdom, to the individual at his best. For what else than the advancement of the individual is it that he proposes for him a "best self, and right reason which may stand as a

serious authority?" The state, or whatever
higher power it may be, is to stand as the indi-
vidual should stand at his best; it is to stand
against his caprice, is to stand for him, is
to be his *very* self, — his right, his best, self.
"We see then," he says, "how indispensable to
that human perfection which we seek is, in the
opinion of good judges [Renan and Wilhelm
von Humboldt], some public recognition and
establishment of our best self, or right reason."
Whether the plan prove feasible or not,
Arnold's intent is anything but "against the
individual." The state having been supreme in
Greece, it is easy to attribute Arnold's view of
the individual to his Hellenism, and, having
styled his view Hellenic, it is easy to make it
square with the old Greek view; but it is once
more pressing Arnold's Hellenism too hard. If
to bear down so heavily on Arnold's Hellenism
is to misread him, to transfer a distorted politi-
cal opinion to the distant domains of religion,
literature, and art, to say that his regard for

institutionalism " makes him indifferent to the
element of personalism, the flavor of character,
the quality of unique individual genius, where-
ever found in art, literature, or religion " —
this is misinterpretation indeed.

Nor can we discover in Arnold's writings
ground for the statement that his strictures
against the dissenter spring from the fact that
the "dissenter stands for personal religion,
religion as a private and individual experience."
The gist of the teaching so warmly advocated
in "Literature and Dogma" is religion as a
personal experience. Israel's old sure proof of
being in the right way — the sanction of joy and
peace . . . *this was a test which anybody could
at once apply.* Again, Christ came to "restore
the intuition." What possible way is there of
coming at this sanction of joy and peace except
by personal experience? and what is intuition,
apart from personal experience?

Finally, the observation, " It is clear enough
that [Arnold] would sooner be a Catholic than

a Presbyterian or a Methodist," seems equally
wide of the mark. The critic says elsewhere
that Arnold accords to Protestantism moral su-
periority over Catholicism. In " Literature and
Dogma " Arnold avers that Protestantism has
the most light; and we had thought it beyond
dispute that, notwithstanding a leaning toward
the Catholic Church (he calls it a weakness, by
the way) because of the "rich treasures of
human life which have been stored within her
pale," or a leaning in any other direction, he
ranges himself unmistakably on the side of
morals and light. Other points in this paper
might be examined with a like result; but per-
haps these few are sufficient to illustrate what
we mean by the tendency among Arnold's
critics to stop short of his full meaning.

As before said, just so far as the Greek
stands for intelligence, for the free play of
mind that sees things as they are, and finds life
joyous, beautiful, — just so far is Arnold a
Greek. The laws discovered and obeyed by

the Greeks are interesting to him, not because
they are Greek laws, but because they are ele-
mental laws, basal laws of our being. His
words are very clear here, as elsewhere: "The
generality of men attend only to the indica-
tions of a true law of our being as to conduct;
and hardly at all to indications, though they
as really exist, of a true law of our being on
its æsthetic and intelligential side."

To classify poetry, for example, Arnold
adopts the Greek system; not because it is
Greek, but because it is "natural," elemental.
For the constituents of a true poem, he turns
again to the Greek, as did Goethe and Coler-
idge, for the same reason.

What Arnold takes from Greece, Greece
took from nature herself, — the "natural truth."
Let us drop Hellenism for a time, and substi-
tute elemental laws that lead to intelligence, to
clear seeing. "The power of intellect and
science," he says, "the power of beauty, the
power of social life and manners, — these are

what Greece so felt, and fixed, and may stand
for. They are great elements in our humani-
zation." Very true, but, "The power of con-
duct is another great element; and this was so
felt and fixed by Israel that we can never with
justice refuse to permit Israel, in spite of all
his shortcomings, to stand for it."

Very true again, but, "In many respects the
ancients are far above us, and yet there is
something which we demand that they can
never give." If we set out with a thinker, let
us go the whole way. Arnold was not the
blind worshipper of the ancients that the fancy
of the impatient reviewer has painted.

We have travelled beyond the pale of litera-
ture. This was unavoidable; for literature
with the author of "Literature and Dogma" is
but a part of the great whole of life. Arnold,
then, tried by the highest standard, is a great
critic; a critic in the largest sense of the word,
a critic of life. He is a great critic because he
brings to bear on a variety of great subjects,

extensive knowledge, superior power of perception, and clear, pure, adequate utterance. To this equipment must be added signal patience and gentleness of temper. Sober, painstaking, he builds on a few primal laws.

Instead of trying to decide whether Arnold accomplished more in this field or in that, or whether he covered all the ground in each field, it would seem wiser to ascertain what he did accomplish in each field, and, better still, to learn the sum of his discoveries. The first step with him was to insist on knowledge before forming belief, before rendering an opinion. It is not the admonition of a theorist, but of a worker, one who gave by choice a great part of his time and strength to the toil of an inspector of schools; one who sought the thing he pronounced indispensable, and who, as he sought, put what he found into practical working: —

"His life he to his doctrine brought."

Arnold approached life from many sides ; some-

times a literary critic, sometimes a poet, he
is always a moralist, a teacher, urging the
world in his frank, captivating way, to reach
toward the higher life.   The catholicity of
his research, his freedom from trammels of
race, of age, of sect, taught him that truths,
wherever found, cannot conflict.   His aim, his
service, was not to found a system; it was to
establish rules of inquiry regarding the requi-
sites for a high, full life.   He knew his limita-
tions, and accepted them.   "The best that is
known and thought in the world" — get that,
he says, make it your own and act on it, and
the best is done that can be done.   With this
maxim as a constant monitor, he endowed criti-
cism with unwonted seriousness, dignity, gra-
ciousness, and trustworthiness.   He did more;
lifting pure criticism as near perhaps as it may
rise to the plane of creative art, he spread
abroad the spiritual and intellectual influences
of receptivity and support, without which crea-
tive art finds itself at a cruel disadvantage, if,

indeed, it be not baffled.   If he lacks in enthusiasm, he is no less earnest than serene.   His effect is not that of a sudden dawn of enlightenment; the process is slower and surer, being a gradual expansion, a steady widening of the mental and spiritual horizon.   Of Arnold, first of all, it may be said, *He clears away the mists.* Neither a prophet nor a lawgiver, he is a restorer of neglected laws which have been since time was, primal principles which are from everlasting to everlasting.   In religion, in art, his plea is for the absolute and eternal.   Nor does it cease at the door of politics : —

"Perfection will never be reached; but to recognize a period of transformation when it comes, and to adapt themselves honestly and rationally to its laws, is perhaps the nearest approach to perfection of which men and nations are capable.   No habits or attachments should prevent their trying to do this; nor, indeed, in the long run, can they.   Human thought, which all institutions are, inevitably saps them, resting only in that which is absolute and eternal."

How large the view is, how clear the vision, the judgment how sane! Here is a writer that writes for something besides writing's sake; a writer that finds the great man greater than the great prose writer, or the great poet; a high priest of culture that lodges his country's hope in the stiff-necked Puritan middle class.

Before taking a final glance at Arnold as an apostle of doubt, so called, a word concerning his style, the secret of which, the critics generally seem to have missed. "Without range and force of thought, all the resources of style, whether in cadence or in subtlety, are not and can not be brought out." Here is the key to his style, warm from his own hand. A delicate sense, a fine ear, can produce polished writing; for great writing must be added "range and force of thought." Should this truth be desired in concrete form, one has but to read the author of "The Reverberator" on Arnold, then Arnold on Milton. Arnold's style is the result of knowledge, of thought power; this first, then patient, intelligent training of the artist's instinct. So nicely fitted is the word to the thought that, when a thought is to be exactly repeated, the exact word first used must be used again. Writers opulent as he are not afraid to borrow the words of another, nor do they fear to face their own words a second time. It is for the sake of the thought *and* euphony that the synonym is so often rejected. The thought is given a name that rings in the ear because of its fitness as well as of its music; it must not be lost, for it cannot be replaced. . . . " To walk in awful observance of an *enduring clew*, within us and without us, which leads to happiness " —there is no other way to say this as well. Arnold's oft-rung phrases, instead of affectations, are formulated truths with catchwords, which, once caught, cling like burrs. They evidence, not trickery, but close knowledge, of the sort that caused Emerson to set so

highly by nicknames. Temperament enters into
the material of style; and when we consider the
nature of the faults Arnold pointed out, there is
little room for censure. Sharp as his strictures
may be, he never, like the mighty " organ-voice "
when pamphleteering; or, like the fervent, dys-
peptic Scotsman, so lately gone, when dealing
with other than his hero ; or, like the art critic
still indulging his wayward moods, lashing
right and left with his whip of thongs, — he
never, like these, tries titles with the common
scold. His earnestness is always accompanied
by a governing sobriety ; hence, the dissenter
listens respectfully. The man so admirable as
a coadjutor is winning even to his opposers.
He may say to-day, and again to-morrow, you
have "need of conduct, need of beauty, need
of knowledge, need of manners "; he may go a
smart step further and call names, — *Philistine!*
Barbarian! but behind all is plainly to be seen
the gentle man, the generous helper, the amiable
lover of wisdom.

Arnold insists on intelligence for the right seeing of what may be termed the secular phenomena of life ; crossing into the domain of religion, he demands the same there. The intelligence commended is on its way hither, and he is convinced that certain old religious beliefs cannot stand before it. With the fall of these may go down, for the hour, much that should remain, must remain in the fulness of time, and he gives warning : —

"But at the present moment two things about the Christian religion must surely be clear to anybody with his eyes in his head. One is, that men cannot do without it; the other, that they cannot do with it as it is."

This is not an original discovery. We are indebted to Arnold for presentations of this and other familiar facts in a light so clear that they seem new; for a marshalling of wise words, conciliatory as admonitory, in a wholly fresh order and beauty of array. We have in him a teacher that can take what is good from

Catholic and from Protestant, from Christian and from Pagan, from yesterday and from to-day. We have in him a counsellor who has sought widely and deeply, given up his splendid powers mainly to one aim, — the ascertaining of the best that has been told, and the recasting of selections from it, in accordance with the dictates of his rich mental and spiritual equipment and with the need of the time. We may listen to this counsellor; he is in earnest, he has our good at heart, and his stature makes him one to be looked up to. Now, what does he say about the Bible, about religion, and about Christ? dismissing critics and interpreters, what are his own words?

"When the Bible is read aright, it will be found to deal, in a way incomparable for effectiveness, with facts of experience most pressing, momentous, real."

Again, "Protestantism has hold of Christ's method of inwardness and sincerity; Catholicism has hold of his 'secret' of self-renouncement. . . . Neither has his unerring balance, his intuition, his *sweet reasonableness.*"

Again, " Christianity is truly . . . the greatest and happiest stroke ever yet made for human perfection."

Again, "And therefore it is so all-important to insist on what I call the *natural truth* of Christianity. . . . Jesus Christ and his precepts are found to hit the moral experience of mankind, to hit it in the critical points, to hit it lastingly."

Again, " And a certainty is the sense of *life*, of being truly *alive*, which accompanies righteousness, . . . and here we may well permit ourselves to trust Jesus."

Does not our apostle of doubt here write himself down a disciple of belief? Because some things in the Christian religion cannot be believed, he says, you are letting all go. There is a wiser way. Better too much belief than too little; but certain things in the Christian religion you must believe, and they are valuable beyond comparison. One critic, with well nigh wicked quickness, has leaped to the conclusion that the master-work, "Literature and Dogma," was written to carry Christianity over into the Roman camp. The author himself says, it "was written in order to win access for the Bible and its religion to many of those who now neglect them. . . . To people disposed to throw the Bible aside, 'Literature and Dogma' sought to restore the use of it." The aim is again declared in "God and the Bible."

"But 'Literature and Dogma' had altogether for its object, and so, too, has the present work, to show the truth and necessity of Christianity, and its power and charm for the heart, mind, and imagination of man, even though the preternatural, which is now its popular sanction, should be given up."

We have come to the gist of the matter, the elimination of the preternatural. This is not the place to attempt a discussion of the fate of

the preternatural in Christianity. We may say
simply that Arnold, believing, with many of the
foremost thinkers of the time, that its days are
well nigh numbered; seeing, indeed, unmis-
takable evidence of its elimination, urges the
acceptance of the surpassingly worthy residue
to which men can still cling, to which they
must cling do they lay claim to wisdom, to
common-sense, to even the crudest reasonable-
ness, do they have any hope of genuine hap-
piness. This is no doubter's *rôle*; it is the
rôle of a believer, one come to the deliverance
of doubters. Whether the postulate, "the
Eternal, who makes for righteousness," suf-
fices, is open to question; but the admirable
method of inquiry, the rules for patient, pure,
high, full living, which are the foundation
of "Literature and Dogma," do not admit of
argument. Because one doubts, one is not
necessarily without faith. Arnold has faith;
not this faith, nor that, perhaps, but his
own. No soul strives after the fashion of his

without hope. He cannot see all that others have professed, and that others still profess, to see; but hope is in him, if not glowing, yet rational and strong. He sees other than brilliant colors ; but surely life has sober hues, and he was a student of life. The man that reaches downward as tenderly as did he to the dumb animal must feel a higher hand than his own reaching down to him. It is true that Arnold, with the first scientist and with the first poet of his time, cannot believe all that has been, and yet is, believed; it is true that he leans back hard on renouncement; but it is equally true that he is strong in hope, that he is unshaken in faith, and true also that he can give a reason for the faith that is in him. He meets darkness, he finds a line, indeed, where hope must stop, must stay on this side; still the darkness is rayed with the " light " always in his spirit and so often on his tongue, and checked hope pauses, content, to wait for the knowledge of the morrow : —

> " And though we wear out life, alas!
> Distracted as a homeless wind,
> In beating where we must not pass,
> In seeking what we shall not find;
>
> Yet we shall one day gain, life past,
> Clear prospect o'er our being's whole;
> Shall see ourselves, and learn at last
> Our true affinities of soul."

Only strong hope sees the future for the world that he predicts. Still staking his all on knowledge, intelligence, and valor, he says, —

" A clearing and enlarging spirit is in the air; all the influences of the time help it. . . . The one way to prevent or adjourn its working is to keep education what is called a hole-and-corner affair."

All life except the aimless, the grovelling, is well worth living : —

> " How fair a lot to fill
> Is left to each man still! "

Of a truth, Arnold is a man of sorrows; but his are not the griefs that force one into ignoble

behavior.   We may address him, as fitly as he
did the gypsy child, in the beautiful words, —

"Thy sorrow and thy calmness are thine own:
Glooms that enhance and glorify this earth."

He is a man of sorrows, he is also a man of
joys.

" To feel that one is fulfilling in *any* way the
law of one's being, that one is succeeding and
hitting the mark, brings us, *we know*, happiness ;
to feel this in regard to so great a thing as
conduct brings, of course, happiness propor-
tionate to the thing's greatness."

Here is the real, the whole Arnold; in the
domain of prose and on Hebrew ground.   Not
in the poems inspired by the Greeks, masterful
as they are, nor yet in his still more masterly
criticism of the Greeks, do we get to the very
heart of the man.   One may say that he hardly
seemed to know this himself, and perhaps it
should not be surprising that so few know it of
him.   Arnold was at his highest when dealing
in prose with the eternal moralities as they

were proclaimed by the impassioned Hebrews, with the glorious outpouring of their "intuition of God." After all his proneness to the poetry of the Greeks, after all, and in spite of, his declarations as to the necessity of leaning upon it for solace, for self-preservation, he really rested upon the poetry of the Hebrews. Not till he reaches that does the weakness, the pessimism disappear, and the full man come forth in his strength. The one inconsistency that we find in him — discussed in our endeavor to answer the question, Who are the Great Poets? — is his reading of the milestones that lead to the poetry of Greece the while his feet are in the path that leads straight to the poetry of Palestine.

Solon, hearing one of Sappho's songs, exclaimed, "I must not die till I have learned the song." Arnold makes of this a text to ring life long in the ears of an indifferent world: *You must not die till you have learned the poet's song.* Milton's great sayings on poetry, and

Wordsworth's greater saying than any of Milton's, that to be without poetry is to be without God — these had been uttered; and Carlyle and Emerson with isolated emphasis were speaking contemporaneously to a like purport; but Arnold stood forth alone to preach without ceasing the gospel of poetry. Though few, very few, critics have approached Arnold's understanding of poetry, his mastery of it from the finest point of technics up to the utmost reach of the power of the art, after all, the distinctive thing to be said of him is that he first proclaimed from day to day and from year to year the evangel of song.

IV

WHAT ABOUT BROWNING?

IV

WHAT ABOUT BROWNING?

Not oo word spak he more than was neede,
And that was seid in forme and reverence.
— *Chaucer.*

WHEN, at the beginning of the present
century, English singers, voicing a protest
against the verse of the century before, reached
toward the drama, one, at least, of the tuneful
rebels obeyed the bent of his genius; for the
Browning of " Paracelsus " is radically the
same Browning found in the " Parleyings."
Now, who and what is Robert Browning in
the literary world? Admitted that he is a
thinker, an original, profound thinker; that
he is a philosopher, an unwearied prober of
man's mind and heart, an untiring, dauntless
searcher among the hidden, mysterious forces of
life, — is he, in addition, a poet, and, if so, how

123

far a poet? Would we pass on Browning, or
another, as a poet, the judgment must be by
the laws of poetry; and the special point here
raised, is, that these laws demand not only the
poet's wisdom and vision, but the poet's utter-
ance, the poet's expression no less than the
poet's conception. Lay what stress we may
on Browning's defective expression, he is a
seer, one that sees the inside, the spirit of
things, — he is a poet; and, wanting in the con-
structive power of the dramatist, he may be
best styled a dramatic poet, with the reminder
that his *dramatis personæ* are objective, are
drawn in the purely dramatic method in char-
acter and situation only, the voice being invari-
ably the voice of Browning. The poet wholly
dramatic is thoroughly objective in method, is
lost in the absorbing personages that come and
go at his bidding; while Browning, though he
enter into both the substance and the situation
with a singular liveliness of sympathy, does not
surrender his resistless individuality. Be it

scoundrel or saint, the turn of expression, the *ictus*, is Browning's. The work is strong, intensely forcible when at its highest, but the writer's persistent personality divides honors with the imaginary speaker to whom we would give undivided attention. We cannot let go the adjective dramatic, neither can we retain it unqualified.

To go back to first principles, if we abide by the Miltonic *dictum* — poetry is "simple, sensuous, passionate" — rarely can we put our finger down and say, here Browning is a poet. If we square by the old rule — old as poetry itself, though formulated anew by Matthew Arnold — "the noble and profound application of ideas to life is the most essential part of poetic greatness," though every page be crowded with ideas, these always prying at some unyielding root of life, we are little better off; for the application must be "under the conditions immutably fixed by the laws of poetic beauty and poetic truth." First principles bid us bear in mind this much, if no more : poetry is the kind of writing that is not prose, with a charm of its own and an unmistakable, imperishable individuality.

On Burke's authority, Sheridan's eloquence was something better than either prose or poetry, but, inasmuch as we are not informed what the something was, we are obliged to keep to the old two divisions; and such is the confusion abroad that we must insist on the absolute independence of these divisions, the one of the other, affirming that poetry is always poetry, and prose always prose. Furthermore, strange as it may seem, it has become necessary to restate the old truth that the various kinds of poetry, differ widely as they may, have in common qualities — imagination, method or manner of thought, suggestive force, atmosphere, music — that serve emphatically for classification as song; in other words, that they reveal at once, together with their several characteristics, their kinship, their membership of one family.

Were it the design to establish a high position for Browning as a poet, among his shorter pieces " Childe Roland " would prove, perhaps, the happiest selection. The imagination is strong, the creative power strikingly manifest; while the treatment of the favorite motto, " Push forward on your own lines," comes unwontedly near to fulfilling the demands of a noble poem. The wandering line of the fool could suggest a poem to no other than a genuine poet, and could suggest such a poem to a poet of a high order only. The mystic union of nature and the spirit of man under fearful conditions overlapping the bounds between the natural and the supernatural, invests the composition with an atmosphere akin to that of — solitary creation in the realm of marvel! — the " Ancient Mariner."

> " As for the grass, it grew as scant as hair
> In leprosy; thin dry blades pricked the mud
> Which underneath looked kneaded up with blood.
> One stiff blind horse, his every bone a-stare,
> Stood stupefied, however he came there:
> Thrust out past service from the devil's stud!

Alive? he might be dead for aught I know,
With that red gaunt and colloped neck a-strain,
And shut eyes underneath the rusty mane;
Seldom went such grotesqueness with such woe;
I never saw a brute I hated so;
He must be wicked to deserve such pain."

There is the Coleridgian imagination — minus the music. The fact that " Childe Roland " has marched so well toward the rear in the line of favor may be excusably adduced as one item of proof that the disciples of Browning follow their lord rather through all the world than into the thin air of song.

After " Childe Roland," " Andrea del Sarto " presents, from the poet's stand-point, perhaps the strongest claim for admiration. The dark side, so tempting to Browning, is turned toward us, but streaked by a glorious light. Were it possible to forget " Evelyn Hope " and certain lines that spring to mind at the mention of " By the Fireside," " Andrea del Sarto," of itself, would put it beyond dispute that Browning *can* be simple, sweet, delightful.

" But had you — oh, with the same perfect brow,
  And perfect eyes, and more than perfect mouth,
  And the low voice my soul hears, as a bird
  The fowler's pipe, and follows to the snare —
  Had you, with these the same, but brought a mind!
  Some women do so."

Were Browning always what he is in "Childe Roland," in "Andrea del Sarto," in "Fra Lippo Lippi," and "My Last Duchess," — not to name such longer poems as "Pippa Passes" and "A Blot in the 'Scutcheon," — what he is there in kind if not in degree, we should be spared our ineffectual scepticism and — the Societies. It is because, at one time, he is content with mere ingenuity, dropping to out-and-out juggling, indulging in preposterous hodge-podge; because, at another time, he fails to distinguish between metaphysic, psychologic disquisition and poetry, between cacophonic cataloguing and the direct, swift, entrancing measures of song; because he is not averse from veiling his concepts with word mists all but impenetrable, his skill running to encysted

intricacies — linkèd riddles long drawn out;
because in drawing his pains through rhyme's
vexation he draws them through our own;
because he commonly disobeys the kind laws
that have helped him to his enviable height, as
they have helped the great singers of all ages,
— it is for these reasons, among others, that we
hesitate to pronounce Robert Browning from
first to last a poet, —

> " Steadfast and rooted in the heavenly muse,
> And washed and sanctified to Poesy."

The fiery Pegasus is turned and wound up
and down many a page; but the angel is not in
the saddle, the world is not witched. We may
cheerfully, enthusiastically, grant the poet's
heart always, often the poet's head; but the
poet's voice, save in rare calls, no.

Those of Browning's readers that have not
progressed beyond the stage of the beautiful in
art, must be aware that he has, too, a fondness
for subjects unpleasant, not to say repelling.
Perhaps it was unfortunate in this particular

that the poet exposed himself so early in his
career to the sanguinary saturation of Italian
life. Were he more a Briton in his books, we
should escape not a little intrigue and very
un-English obliquity.

Reference has been made to a questionable
substitution of vivisection for verse, of meta-
physics for metre and rhythm, and to a prevail-
ing opaqueness; now let us take our bearings,
and, laying a little firmer hold of our first prin-
ciples, see if we can indicate what part of
Browning's important gift to the world is
poetry.

For sound, wholesome advice on the subject
of poetry we may turn confidently to Cole-
ridge; a metaphysician, too, by the way, but
never when in his singing robes. This master
among poets and critics, says : —

" But if the definition sought for be that of a
legitimate poem, I answer, it must be one, the
parts of which mutually support and explain
each other; all in their proportion harmonizing

with, supporting, the purpose and known influences of metrical arrangement. The philosophic critics of all ages coincide with the ultimate judgment of all countries, in equally denying the praises of a just poem, on the one hand, to a series of striking lines or distichs, each of which absorbing the whole attention of the reader to itself, disjoins it from its context, and makes it a separate whole, instead of a harmonizing part; and on the other hand, to an unstained composition, from which the reader collects rapidly the general result unattracted by the component parts. The reader should be carried forward, not merely or chiefly by the mechanical impulse of curiosity, or by a restless desire to arrive at the final solution; but by the pleasurable activity of mind excited by the attractions of the journey itself."

The most superficial reader must detect the unevenness of Browning's work. Single verses and groups of verses shine and blossom, very jewels in a heap of sand, lovely roses " emongst

the wicked weeds." An instance of these iso-
lated excellencies is the extension of Sir
Thomas Browne's "The circle of our felici-
ties makes but short arches," in the splendid
line, —

"On the earth the broken arcs; in the heaven, a perfect
round."

After all, Browning's writing goes best in the
bulk; it is the general result that we enjoy,
being oftener rather distracted than attracted
by the component parts. And it is too true
that, as a rule, we miss, with the mutual sup-
port and explanation, the "known influences of
metrical arrangement." Consequently, though
curiosity be roused, we journey much of the
way unaccompanied by the pleasure Coleridge
commends and commands; we feel the grasp of
a strong hand, but it is not the hand of the
enchanter. Now, if these touchstones be gen-
uine, and properly applied in the present case,
it is evident that only here and there in Brown-
ing's work, virile, inspiring, as it is, may we

find a "legitimate," a "just," poem. As before
stated, the poet must be judged by the laws of
poetry; and the purpose of this paper will be
achieved if by it any student of poetry, whether
sought in Browning or another, be persuaded
to make sure, first, that he takes the poetry
road, not the prose road, then that he sets out
with the right foot, the poetic foot, forward, not
the left foot, the philosophic foot. If the
intent be to get the surest word spoken on
poetry, counsel will be taken of authorities
on the laws of poetry; application will be
made to a Coleridge of yesterday, or to an
Arnold, Lowell, Stoddard, or Stedman of to-
day. This, for such information from the posi-
tive concurrence of the ages as appertains
strictly to poetry. Now we make bold to say
that this *consensus* approves the following three
propositions : first, that immediate theory,
direct philosophy, is most difficult, most dan-
gerous in poetry, fatal in the hands of all save
the greatest poets; second, that poetry and

beauty are inseparable; third,'that the maxim
of White of Selborne, "As long as there is any
incubation going on, there is music," is as true
in poetry as in ornithology.   Great Words-
worth and greater Milton have taught us the
distinction between naked philosophy and
poetry, and between naked and flayed theology
and poetry, by sadly practical illustrations.
Plainly, it is possible for an old traveller to
lose the poetry road, and

> " He needs must wander that has lost his way."

He must wander, and he may flounder.

But, the small morals of verse wanting, we
are told that Browning discards them for the
massive keys of life.   If Browning's keys open
to things "essential and eternal in the heart,"
why are they so unwieldy in the master hand?
If his gates open to the white realm of life, why
should they grate, much as did the black bar-
riers that threatened Erebus?

> " . . . leaving truth,
> And virtue, difficult, abstruse and dark;
> Hard to be won, and only by a few;

> Strange should He deal herein with nice respects,
> And frustrate all the rest! Believe it not;
> The primal duties shine aloft — like stars;
> The charities that soothe, and heal, and bless,
> Are scattered at the feet of man — like flowers.
> The generous inclination, the just rule,
> Kind wishes, and good actions, and pure thoughts —
> No mystery is here."

If no mist shrouds the deep of primal duties, will the " religious poet of the future " sound them with a fog-horn?

> " Is thy strait horizon dreary ?
>   Is thy foolish fancy chill ?
> Change the feet that have grown weary
>   For the wings that never will.
> Burst the flesh and live the spirit;
>   Haunt the beautiful and far;
> Thou hast all things to inherit,
>   And a soul for every star."

Here is didacticism pure and simple, still it is poetry. Here is plain advice, plain English as well, still it is the *vera vox*.

" The very essence of truth," says Milton, " is plainness and brightness." Browning pays little court to these, little court to beauty. " No beauty to be had but in wresting and writhing our own tongue"? Rare Ben's question acquires the accent of prophecy. Indifference to beauty is a serious defect; in poetry it is an offence, only less heinous than the sacrifice of clearness. If a literary composition have not perspicuity and some sort of beauty, the remaining virtues have a task before them to save it to poetry. "The first law of art, the law of beauty," says Lessing. "In poetry," says Lowell, "language is something more than merely the vehicle of thought; . . . if there is a beauty of use, there is often a higher use of beauty." Heretofore the testimony has been on the side of beauty.

Music is an element of beauty; and Coleridge's words, before quoted, are, the "known influences of metrical arrangement." This point, with Coleridge, is one long definitely settled. Elsewhere he uses, perhaps, the most remarkable language yet spoken on the value of music in verse: "The sense of musical delight with the power of producing it, is a

gift of the *imagination.*" Here, music is not
a happy attachment to the creative faculty, but
is of the very stuff of it. It is not merely orna-
mental, it is integral, vital. Very well; granting,
for the moment, that Browning's work fulfils all
the other demands of poetry, is it, as a whole,—

" The word of the Poet by whom the deeps of the world
   are stirred,
The music that robes it in language beneath and beyond
   the word "?

If the answer be in the negative, it is not, as a
whole, poetry; much less poetry of the better
class, which, in consideration of the source, it
must be if poetry at all. Listen! there is
whispering among our first principles: " Opu-
lent in thought as Browning is, ' rich ' as he is
' with the spoils of time,' he is poor in speech;
the occasion being rare when he commands the
befitting, the indispensable, the indisputable
delivery of the sons of song." Browning's
flashing scalpel is turned on his own energetic
intellectuals, and it is hinted that he has what
Hawthorne terms " too much of one sort of

brain, and hardly any of another." So close, so singular, is his thinking, the whispering goes on, that it would be hard enough to follow him were the expression clear; but when to the difficulty of the thought is added abrupt, elliptical language, tearing its way in torrents, the reader that is not an athlete ceases to pursue out of sheer fatigue.

Not a few good minds and true lend a willing ear to our saucy intangibles. These speak still more boldly, saying not only that they cannot follow Browning as a poet, but that they must stand and shudder at such bruising of song's flowerets with the armed hoof of hostile paces. They declare that the limits of the human mind are no longer respected, that patience is strained even to its undoing; that they are beset with too many metrical pieces, with too much in one piece, yes, with too much, altogether too much, in each piece of a piece : —

> " Huge trunks! and each particular trunk a growth
> Of intertwisted fibres serpentine,
> Up-coiling, and inveterately convolved."

Was it fancy? or did we catch even a cry, Give
us once more the old Homeric nod! We cer-
tainly heard, —

> " A thousand circlets spread
> And each misshape the other."

In one who has shown so little capacity for
improvement in art, our old-fashioned, out-
spoken friends find that the tendency towards
verbosity and obscurity has naturally increased
with years, till " Ferishta's Fancies " and the
" Parleyings " and their congeners are but
whirlwinds of disquisitory dust. The lovers
of the old poetry and censors of the new, pass-
ing from the form to the matter, leave us to
infer that they are not so sure of getting from
the sower of the " Red Cotton Night-Cap
Country " garden more lettuce than nettles.
They cannot make certain that Browning strikes
habitually to the heart of wisdom. They are
positive of singularly spirited displays of singu-
lar mental situations, of an astonishing extol-
ment of the odd, a deification of the queer;

beyond this they seem to be unable to go.
Finally, there is a *consensus* of opinion, among
the blunt old-time dissenters, that mental gym-
nastics the very cleverest, keenest analysis,
most skilful vivisection and psychologic prob-
ing, subtlest casuistry, daring speculation, daz-
zling wealth of learning, humor, satire, fire
truly volcanic, all these combined — as, indeed,
they are, to-day, in this one author and in him
only — do not make a poet; poetry being the
" *blossom*, the *fragrancy* of all human knowl-
edge, human passion, emotion, language," — a
very different thing from the root, stalk,
branches, or even the leaves, of these mar-
vellous plants. Persistent wilfulness, habitual
disobedience to the primal laws of simplicity
and beauty — this cloud tormentingly lowers as
they turn the thousand pages of Browning,
dulling the clear, delightful impression of true
poetry. When they that " have bene watered
at the muses' well " speak, they find that it is
without circumlocution and with no uncertain

sound; and they fear that it is only when the poetic life is gone out that the eagles of explanation are gathered together.

To speak temperately, steering between the extremes of the doubters and the adorers, we may hope to hit a just mean when we affirm that there is this fundamental trouble with the bulk of Browning's writing: his favorite kind of truth is not the poet's kind, and his processes with it are not the poet's processes. Both belong rather to the prose of philosophy and science. The thought is often important, but, whether important or not, it has an alien look in the field of song. The Browning plant is not entirely native, bright, and clean; flower as it may, it has a viscous stalk, thick with the insects of speculation. This, by the bye, is far from saying that the poetic field is not ultimately to be enriched by the Browning growths; like the inedible sedges, the rankest among them may serve to mass the soil, and so prepare firm ground for the sweet food of song. Bright

truths set forth in transfigured words — this
expression certainly does not help to describe
the greater part of Browning's work, the part
of which we speak; it does help to describe the
work of the poet.

Browning's work lacks proportion; it is
wanting in judgment, in taste. The lack of
taste really includes all.

> " Oh, too absurd —
> But that you stand before me as you stand!
> Such beauty does prove something, everything!
> Beauty's the prize-power which dispenses eye
> From peering into what has nourished root —
> Dew or manure: the plant best knows its place.
> Enough, from teaching youth and tending age
> And hearing sermons, — haply writing tracts, —
> From such strange love-besprinkled compost, lo,
> Out blows this triumph!"

The hand that could write this in quiet, needed
only the stimulus of excitement to pen the
notorious twelve lines to Fitzgerald.

An eminent linguist has said that the "poetic
form embodies the highest expression of the
human intellect"; and this may be taken as

the sentiment of the cultured world. The importance of form admitted, it is diverting to see with what ingenuity the point at issue is evaded in the overshadowing presence of the poet under review. An illustrious American singer and critic says, " But if form means the production of that which stimulates and re-enforces thought by powerful emotion, the subsidence of which leaves the thoughts as a *key of life* and a *rule* for conduct, no one has given truer examples of it than Browning." The key to certain phases of life Browning may put in our hand, and — though not always, if we comprehend him — safe rules for conduct; but no one could know better than the author of the words quoted, that they amount simply to an adroit dodge. It is one thing to speak as chairman of a " Browning Society," quite another thing to speak as a free roamer in the literary field. What this same critic says about form as he saunters in the open field, it were hard to better : —

" And we men through our bit of song run,
　Until one just improves on the rest,
　And we call a thing his, in the long run,
　Who utters it clearest and best."

" What to others a trifle appears,
　Fills me full of smiles or tears."

The idea was once Blake's. It is now Words-
worth's : —

" To me the meanest flower that blows can give
　Thoughts that do often lie too deep for tears."

The ground taken by some defenders of
Browning as an artist, that his form is a law
unto itself, is not tenable until it be shown that
their master is more masterly than their mas-
ter's masters, who essentially agree among
themselves, and with whom he does not agree.

How used it to sound? Let us hear it once
more — the happy accent of the old masters : —

" Monsters unnatural! you that have been covetous
　Of your own father's death, gape you for mine now ?
　Cannot a poor old man, that now can reckon
　Even all the hours he has to live, live quiet,
　For such wild beasts as these, that neither hold
　A certainty of good within themselves,

> But scatter others' comforts that are ripen'd
> For holy uses ? is hot youth so hasty,
> It will not give an old man leave to die,
> And leave a widow first, but will make one,
> The husband looking on ?   May your destructions
> Come all in hasty figures to your souls ! "

Again : —

> " My father oft would speak
> Your worth and virtue, and as I did grow
> More and more apprehensive, I did thirst
> To see the man so prais'd; but yet all this
> Was but a maiden-longing, to be lost
> As soon as found; till sitting in my window,
> Printing my thoughts in lawn, I saw a god
> I thought (but it was you) enter our gates;
> My blood flew out, and back again as fast,
> As I had puff'd it forth and suck'd it in
> Like breath; then was I call'd away in haste
> To entertain you.   Never was a man,
> Heav'd from a sheep-cote to a sceptre, rais'd
> So high in thoughts as I; you left a kiss
> Upon these lips then, which I mean to keep
> From you forever; I did hear you talk,
> Far above singing ; after you were gone
> I grew acquainted with my heart, and search'd
> What stirr'd it so: Alas! I found it Love."

Is it not like coming from a conservatory
into the open air ?   The longing maiden, as the
old poet saw her, could print her thoughts in

lawn as a pastime. Think of the task had she come within ken of the author of " Two in the Campagna " ! The dear little thing would be still at it, —

> " With fingers weary and worn,
> With eyelids heavy and red,"

her needles turned divining-rods, the letters grown hieroglyphs, and the virgin lawn stretching away from her virgin lap into interminable space.

We cannot help feeling that the old-stylers are right in the opinion that certain things in this mutable world are pretty well fixed, after all; among them, the few underlying principles of literature, whether verse or prose. In our appeal to authority (for such, not originality, is the aim of this paper) going no further back than 1589, let us call up old George Puttenham, author of " The Arte of English Poesie." " Six points," he says, "set downe by our learned forefathers for a generall regiment of all good utterance, be it by mouth or by writing." It must have "decent proportion"; "it ought to be voluble upon the tongue, and tunable to the eare"; it must not be "tediously long"; it must be of an "orderly and good construction"; it must be "sound, proper, and naturall speech"; it should be "lively and stirring."

Coleridge speaks plainly, while the older lawgiver passes a severe sentence: a large proportion of Browning's work is shut out, not only from the presence of poetry but, from the precincts of "good utterance." Browning need follow no predecessor in the application of the fixed laws of poetic utterance, but he must apply these laws in some way; he must establish the kinship. Where he does this, he is a poet; where he does not do this, whatever else he may be, he is not a poet. The judgment here formed is, that he often fails in this particular; hence, that only a part, the smaller part, of his writing can be called "just," "legitimate," poetry.

Though the two be dissimilar enough, Browning has many points in common with Byron. Both build on the strong foundation of common-sense; both have a fondness for foreign themes, and their literary appetites crave the flavor of the forbidden fruit; both are followers of the off-hand method, the one frequently mistaking oratory for poetry, the other talk for song; and neither fosters the precious faculty that tells what to omit and when to stop. Byron's fame is paying the penalty: posterity is busy weeding and whittling. Again, thought on this vigorous man-of-the-world writer, oddly enough, calls up the thin, mild visage of our revered Concord recluse. Both are poets, both are teachers, both struggle when it comes to the poetic utterance; though it must be said that the success of Emerson in his crystal intervals of emancipation, is beyond the reach of even the Browning of forty years ago. Yet again, between Browning and a third brother is a still more striking family likeness. Fully

as robust, fully as neglectful of form, fully as
intent on the promulgation of a gospel, fully
as positive and stanch, marching at the head
of his following of apologists, is this brother
number three — or, better, number one — who,
lounging on Yankee grass, sends his "yawp"
over the roofs of the world.   Let the lawgivers
of the " poetry of the future " name the strains
of these mighty pipers as they may, those of us
cabined in the present — " bound in to saucy
doubts and fears " — can fasten the fact that
they two are of one blood.

Browning's awkwardness, abruptness, and
obscurity are said to spring from a desire for
condensation. Well, waiving the more prob-
able cause, congenital anfractuosity of intellect,
how is condensation best effected ? Is it by
omitting the parts of speech indispensable to a
complete sentence, or by focusing the thought
in few words? To borrow from Hazlitt, is it
by the decomposition of prose that we arrive at
the composition of poetry ? Browning con-

denses by the phrase, elaborates by the volume.
For example, to set forth the lesson that we
should lead a full life, and, having so done,
be ready to rest, he will write perhaps a book;
while a true economist in expression teaches
the same lesson in four verses : —

> " I strove with none, for none was worth my strife;
>   Nature I loved, and, next to Nature, Art;
> I warmed both hands before the fire of life;
>   It sinks, and I am ready to depart."

That is true condensation; moreover, good
English, the result of pure art — simple, direct,
beautiful. One cannot let go such a quatrain;
it stands, a " Mecca of the mind." Gray, too,
aimed at condensation, but what does he couple
with it? "Extreme conciseness of expression,"
he says, " yet pure, perspicuous, and musical."
And what does Coleridge couple with conden-
sation? His words are, " Boundless fertility,
and labored condensation of thought, with per-
fection of sweetness in rhythm and metre —
these are the essentials in the budding of a

great poet. Afterward habit and consciousness
of power teach more ease — *præcipitandum li-
berum spiritum*." Comparatively few of Brown-
ing's verses linger in memory; had he the power
of artistic, of true condensation, it would be
otherwise.

Much is said about Browning's emotional
nature. He *is* rich in emotion, as he is in intel-
lect, but the same obstacle in the way of his
taking the reader's mind confronts him when
his goal is the reader's heart; and it has grown
to even more formidable proportions. It is
clear, interesting thought, spoken with the
" golden cadence," that starts the flesh creeping
as we read; the golden cadences are

> " The golden keys that ope
> The sacred, sympathetic source of tears."

One of the sincerest of Browning's admi-
rers, speaking of his style, uses the adjective
"chatty." This seems to us a decidedly happy
hit.

Browning's Letters and Chats — perhaps that

were not a bad title for much of the work now labelled so thoroughly, so prodigiously. Right admirable letters and chats they are, for the most part; poetic, too, at times; but poetry —the very titles forbid it. Women chat, men chat; but the muses, if they drop to it, it is after a fashion no nearer our own than that of " The Talking Oak." The familiar quality, the hail fellow well met, the slap on the shoulder element, is very strong in Browning; an evidence of good nature, of warm sympathy, of delightful comradeship, but hardly the evidence to advance the claim of the artist. Art, the most genial, smacks of the aristocratic; art, the most benevolent, gentle, sympathetic, maintains a certain austerity. The muses, though they draw very near, never suffer us to put our hands on them; many may believe it a personal experience, but no man has held Beauty herself in his arms.

As has been said, there is a tendency, at present, to blur the sharp line dividing prose from verse. The fence is down, for example, between Sir Thomas Browne, De Quincey, Carlyle, Ruskin, and the field of song. Truly enough Ruskin's characteristic tribute to the mosses comes closer to poetry than many a page of Browning, yet it is simply prose. Ruskin, a consummate master of style, never forgets that poetry is a different thing from prose; that it has a longer and a higher reach, that it has a subtile inexplicable power which prose may not hope to attain. All his descriptive writing put together, he says, is not worth three lines of Tennyson.

That Browning crosses and recrosses the dividing line between poetry and prose, is proven by the fact that much of his work loses little or nothing, in fact gains, by passing back, here and there, into pure prose, the prose of a sympathetic, scholarly interpreter. The obscurity, the circuitous crudeness and the hair-splitting make welcome an abbreviated, straight-forward, half-prose rendering; and we need look for no further proof that work of which this may be truly said, is devoid of poetic form, if not of poetic substance, and, consequently, is not poetry.

"Whatever lines," says Coleridge, "can be translated into other words of the same language, without diminution of their significance, either in sense or association, or in any other feeling, are so far vicious in their diction." . . . "That *ultimatum* which I have ventured to propose as the infallible test of a blameless style; namely, its untranslatableness in words of the same language without injury to the meaning."

A scholarly expositor may give us, in terms half and half of poetry and prose, the gist of the advocate's argument in the "Ring and the Book," and we will thank him, perhaps; but we would emphatically excuse him from a corresponding version of the lines from the old dramatists before quoted. The poet suffers no man or thing to come between him and the reader.

And this brings us back to the sign-manual of the poet's perfect work — beauty.

In the midst of the present useless and distressing struggle to twist poetry from what it is and ever must be, we shall do well to listen once more to the simple, direct, manly, language of the noblest poet of our American soil : —

"Poetry is that art which selects and arranges the symbols of thought in such a manner as to excite it the most profoundly and delightfully. . . . I suppose that poetry differs from prose, in the first place, by the employment of metrical harmony. It differs from it, in the next place, by excluding all that disgusts, all that tasks and fatigues the understanding, and all matters which are too trivial and common to excite any emotion whatever. . . . To me it seems that one of the most important requisites for a great poet is a luminous style. The elements of poetry lie in natural objects, in the vicissitudes of human

life, in the emotions of the human heart, and
the relations of man to man. He who can
present them in combinations and lights which
at once affect the mind with a deep sense of
their truth and beauty, is the poet for his own
age and the ages that succeed it. It is no dis-
paragement either to his skill or his power that
he finds them near at hand; the nearer they lie
to the common track of the human intelligence,
the more certain is he of the sympathy of his
own generation, and of those which shall come
after him. *The metaphysician, the subtle thinker,
the dealer in abstruse speculations, whatever his
skill in versification, misapplies it when he aban-
dons the more convenient form of prose and per-
plexes himself with the attempt to express his
ideas in poetic numbers.*"

Ay, the fadeless wreath, the eternal benedic-
tion, can never be on the head of metaphysics :—

> " Blessings be with them, and eternal praise,
>   Who gave us nobler loves and nobler cares —
> The poets — who on earth have made us heirs
>   Of truth and pure delight *by heavenly* LAYS."

What is the conclusion? That, if we are to know and respect the poet, we must first know and respect poetry; that, if Browning be not from first to last a poet, he is a poet, and, at his best, a poet of all but the noblest proportions; that, if he be too often, if he be wontedly, lower than the angels of song, he may still have, does have, his own far-raying brightness, shining, now, as one of the resistless forces of his age, destined to shine hereafter, —

" A light and landmark on the cliffs of fame."

All cannot be in any one man. Browning stirs the sluggish blood, rouses the spirit, points out the path to victory. He is a leader in this world where leaders are too few; a very bolt-thrower, sending his hissing missiles into the camp of sham, cowardice, littleness, and all meanness; he is a rounded, complete man; a helper, a teacher, a strong, unfailing friend. All cannot be in any one man: were it not well for the fervor of devoted discipleship to beware the wrong that would crown him that has laurels enough with wreaths he cannot wear?

This for Browning in particular; and generally on the matter of form — for here the discussion hinges — it behooves us not to forget the continuous testimony of the ages to the inexorableness of the august power so lightly set aside. Shall we outgrow the golden cadence? Heaven forbid; for in that day will a thing of beauty be no more a joy; and music, scorning the ground, will have returned to her native height. Personally, we throw in our lot here with the old-stylers, who cannot rejoice in such progress, who cannot believe in it. We do not ask for the old Hebraic ring, or for the clear brook-song of Greece; we avoid the word classic; we rest content with the one simple line of beauty, the eternal curve of the sky, bent graciously over all; we would leave music free as it has been since the beginning in the voice of waters, of birds, and of the air slumbering on

her instrument; we bespeak no special sound
or shape or color of beauty, — but Beauty her-
self we cannot let go. Give us thought, give
us learning, the more the better; but it must be
spoken with the golden cadence, it must bring
the scent and bloom of the upper fields, it must
remind of the features, of the motion, of the
sole glory of the goddess herself, if it would
charm, captivate, the souls of men. On the
shield of song and of art an unwavering hand
has graven the words copied on the shield of
Elpinus, — *I hold by being held.*

V

TENNYSON AND HIS CRITICS

V

TENNYSON AND HIS CRITICS

In a recent communication to the *St. James's Gazette*, Mr. Gosse writes as follows: —

"As we look around us in the Anglo-Saxon world, nay, on the continent of Europe also, we see no living figure which approaches that of Tennyson in literary dignity. . . . This is, perhaps, the moment to ask ourselves why Lord Tennyson and not another is the confessed first man of letters of the present age. In what does his pre-eminence consist? To what qualities of his mind and work does he owe it? No question is more difficult to answer, because the reply depends on the combination of a great number of wholly intangible forces. Still, an answer shall be attempted. In the first place, no pretence is made by the admirers

163

of Lord Tennyson to claim for him eminence
over all his contemporaries in intellect or
knowledge.   He is wise and full of intelli-
gence; but in mere intellectual capacity or
attainment it is probable that there are many
who excel him.   This, then, is not the direction
in which his greatness asserts itself.   He has
not headed a single moral reform, nor inaugu-
rated a single revolution of opinion; he has
never pointed the way to undiscovered regions
of thought; he has never stood on tip-toe to
describe new worlds that his fellows were not
tall enough to discover ahead.   In all these
directions he has been prompt to follow, quick
to apprehend, but never himself a pioneer.
Where, then, has his greatness lain?   It has
lain in the various perfection of his writing."

If the words "all his contemporaries" take
us out of the order of poets, a comparison is
made, here, between things too unlike for
comparison; for, as we have tried to show
elsewhere, often the poet's kind of truth, and

always his intellectual processes in getting at and presenting it, differ from those of other reporters of life. To argue that Tennyson has not headed a moral reform, has not inaugurated a revolution of opinion, does no more toward settling the question of his "intellect or knowledge" than to assert that he has not compiled a volume of the "New English Dictionary," or that he has not met and routed the oratorical forces of Premier Gladstone. If, on the other hand, we are to remain within the circle of poetry, we have simply to reply that the statement, "No pretence is made by the admirers of Lord Tennyson to claim for him eminence over all his contemporaries in intellect or knowledge," is too sweeping. Eminence in intellect and knowledge over his contemporaries in song — we have nothing to do with others — is just what some of us do claim for the laureate. And if asked on what this claim is grounded, we answer, " On his sympathy with essential truths, the poet's truths, the

truths that tell us 'how to live well.'" By
his grasp of these, and by the absence of
attempts to grasp things unessential, to grasp
at things out of mortal reach; in other words,
by his power of discrimination, by the rare
quality of sound judgment on vital questions,
we claim that Tennyson has demonstrated his
superiority in intellect and knowledge to any
English singer of his day, Wordsworth ex-
cepted. What was it Thackeray said to Bayard
Taylor? "Tennyson is the wisest man I
know." And what did Fitzgerald write of the
poet when he was midway in the twenties? "I
felt a sense of depression at times from the
overshadowing of a so much more lofty intel-
lect than my own; this (though it may seem
vain to say so) I never experienced before,
though I have often been with much greater
intellects; but I could not be mistaken in the
universality of his mind; and perhaps I have
derived some benefit in the now more distinct
consciousness of my dwarfishness."

As to the "new worlds" and the "undis-
covered regions of thought," it is not too
much to say that, since the exhaustive dis-
coveries of the ancient Hebrew and Greek
poets, the *great* poets of all lands and times
have found ample room for the play of their
powers in traversing anew and reporting more
in detail, according to the bent of their several
abilities and to the demand of their day, the
regions and worlds they were not the first to
enter, — the domain that every man enters that
is born into time, and that every man must
abide in, whether he will or no, till under cover
of the dismissing shadow he takes his way,
once and for all, out of it. Tennyson, then,
shows his superiority in intellect by refusing to
strain after new regions and new worlds, and
by husbanding his strength for a right interpre-
tation of so much as is interpretable of the
regions and worlds so familiar and yet so
dimly seen. The grand mistake of Tennyson's
most intellectual compeer, has been his standing

on tip-toe for the discovery of new worlds be-
yond the ken of song; this and his neglect of
the requirement of song second only to respect
for its boundary lines, — expression.   He has
stood on his tip-toes, and his followers — beg-
ging their pardon — have stood on their heads;
yet, here we are, in the same old regions, in the
same old worlds.   The great poet is not given
to gymnastics either in thought or in speech;
he simply stands fair and square on his feet.
So Tennyson stands, toe and heel on solid
ground.

A nice balance of noble faculties, whole-
ness of power — this, we take it, indicates
strength of intellect.   There is no crack here
like that, for example, in the brain of lovely
old Cardinal Newman; no twist like that in
the brain of Browning; no abnormal develop-
ment like that in the faculties of Swinburne.
Browning sees, knows, innumerable things, but
his intellect is defective in the part or portion
of it that determines which are the poetic

things; yes, which are the things, whether
for the poet or for the prose writer, for the
man, letters aside, it is worth while to strive
for, to spend time over. Again, when he sees
aright, his tongue, so far as concerns the needs
of poetry, is prone to balk his sight: he sees,
but cannot tell. Swinburne, on the contrary,
limited in vision, has immeasurable utterance.
From Browning we get too much matter, from
Swinburne too little. Tennyson is superior
in intellect to these one-sided poets in that
he is two-sided; to these half-poets in that he
is a whole poet: he discriminates *and* sings, he
sees, knows, *and* tells. While Mr. Gosse is
right in ascribing to Tennyson's work the
quality of "various perfection," this is by no
means taking the measure of the poet. As
cannot be said too many times, "the power of
the poet turns on intellect."

Nor do we think that complete success
attends a like effort of a second eminent
scholar and critic — a wooer of the muse, too

—Professor Dowden. In his essay entitled
" Mr. Tennyson and Mr. Browning," he
says : —

"Mr. Tennyson has a strong sense of the
dignity and efficiency of *law* — of *law* under-
stood in its widest meaning. Energy nobly
controlled, and ordered activity delight his
imagination. Violence, extravagance, immoder-
ate force, the swerving from appointed ends,
revolt — these are with Mr. Tennyson the
supreme manifestations of evil."

This is well said ; and, in his respect for
law, Tennyson does not forget — what we
should least of all forget that he remembers —
the law that governs the poet. It is his respect
for this particular law that has fostered his
genius into the fulness, the luxuriousness, of
its blossoming. But Professor Dowden finds
that respect for law, while it fortunately does
not shut out the idea of God from Tennyson's
poetry, permits only a slight recognition of
"special contact of the soul with the Divine

Being in any supernatural ways of quiet or
of ecstasy." In other words, Tennyson, stand-
ing on the ground of modern science, is "pre-
cluded" from "all spiritual rapture."

We must not decide that Tennyson is defi-
cient in spiritual rapture, or enthusiasm, be-
cause he never lets it overwhelm his judgment
when in the temple of art and in the presence
of his readers. This would be as wrong as to
decide that his reach of mind is short because
he never attempts to soar in regions where
there is no air to stay the wings. Spiritual
rapture, or enthusiasm, is indispensable to the
great poet, but it must be of the right kind.
Sir Thomas Browne, according to Coleridge,
was a "sublime enthusiast, yet a fantast, a
humorist, a brain with a twist." Professor
Dowden gives us the "sublime enthusiast,"
but makes no mention of the important "yet"
and what follows. Enthusiasm has been de-
fined by one that was no stranger to spirit-
ual rapture, as a "divine serenity." It will

hardly be denied that Tennyson has this kind of enthusiasm.

But, suppose for a moment, that Tennyson fails as an enthusiast, moreover that he stands convicted of British insularity, moreover that he lays too little stress on the "distinguished success" of "heroic failure" — suppose these shortcomings and many others proved; may the student of poetry hope to increase his knowledge by heeding a counsellor, never so scholarly, that can compare any lines of Tennyson with such lines as these?

"When liberty goes out of a place it is not the first to go,
      nor the second or third to go,
It waits for all the rest to go — it is the last.
When there are no more memories of heroes and martyrs,
And when all life, and all the souls of men and women are
      discharged from any part of the earth,
Then only shall liberty, or the idea of liberty, be discharged
      from that part of the earth,
And the infidel come into full possession."

This is poetry! This is the sort of composition in which "there is found for the eyes a certain phosphorus, for the taste a certain nectar, for the attention an ambrosia"! This is poetry, and Kinglake's Sphinx nothing but prose!

Incredible as it sounds, the Professor of English Literature in the University of Dublin would have us understand that the liberty lines are poetry. Other critics, distinguished for their attainments, would have us understand the same thing. We must withhold our assent; indeed, we must cry out against this, and ever after view with suspicion the movements of these learned leaders often as they set foot on the poet's ground. When a counsellor in poesy, ay, a poet, can call the liberty lines poetry, can so far forget what poetry is, he can easily fail to discover who is sponsor for it in our time. Next it will be hardly less difficult to find that the laureate's work is to remain to a certain type "futile and false"; not more difficult, in fact, than it is for us to perceive that we are to meet forthwith a doughty champion of Browning — not so much of Browning, the poet, as of Browning, the analyist, the specialist in complex emotions, or Browning, the rhapsodist, the exhorter.

Though Professor Dowden is discussing the philosophy of Tennyson and Browning, he claims to remember that they are " before all else artists "; his avowed aim is to deal with poetry as well as with philosophy. He continues: " As we started with the assumption that Mr. Tennyson has a vivid feeling of the dignity and potency of *law*, let us assume, for the present, that Mr. Browning vividly feels the importance, the greatness and beauty of passions and enthusiasms, and that his imagination is comparatively unimpressed by the presence of law and its operations." We have to read but a page of Browning, perhaps, to be convinced that he is " comparatively," perhaps superlatively, " unimpressed by the presence of law "; it is harder, however, to make sure that he feels deeply the " beauty " of the passions. Unquestionably he has a distinct per-

ception of their "greatness"; but had he as
distinct a perception of their beauty, or of the
beauty of aught else, he would display, as a
poet, a proportional perception of the beauty
of poetic expression, of the loveliness of poetic
utterance. Poetry is no more soul than body,
and the fact that Browning is comparatively
unimpressed by this law of beauty, establishes
at the start his artistic relation to Tennyson.

But setting aside the artist for the philos-
opher, does not Professor Dowden's analy-
sis, after all, support our view of Tennyson's
pre-eminence in intellectuality, in worth, sanity,
wholesomeness? Both Tennyson and Brown-
ing are declared to be optimists, both believe
in the progress of the race; but, while with
Browning this progress is "dependent on the
production of higher passions and aspirations,"
with Tennyson the chief instruments of it are
a "vast increase of knowledge and of political
organization." Important as intuitions and
yearnings are, it would seem safer to look

for progress among the masses of the modern
world through knowledge, gained from long
experience, and wisely applied to their gov-
ernment, than to look for it through the
highest passions and aspirations.   Indeed,
it is not easy to understand how the loftiest
aspirations can make headway, unguided by
sober, plodding knowledge.   The practical
class which, first and last, ask poets what they
teach, are most freakish folk; for the teaching
that pleases them. best is, oddly enough, illy
fitted to the uses of this world.   It may be
excellent for some other world — where, by
the bye, they may have their own poets — but
to be practical for us at present it must serve
upon the humble mother ground.   Thus far,
judgment has been found more useful to the
denizens of earth than has passion; and it
is simply consistent in one that puts the pas-
sions before judgment, to give not a little time
and strength to the laudation of failure.   A
series of failures, if it be operative for instruc-

tion, puts ribs into the suspicion that the
victim is not obeying the safest rules of con-
duct for the world he inhabits.

But we are making a far journey for matter
not as good as we have at home.

"If you miss Browning's psychology," says
Stedman, "you find [in Tennyson] a more
varied analysis, qualified by wise restraint."
Again, "In Tennyson's artistic conscientious-
ness, he is the opposite of that compeer who
approaches him most nearly in years and
strength of intellect."

Of a truth, Tennyson's admirers do claim for
him superiority in intellect and in knowledge
over his contemporaries in song, one and all;
and the reason for their claim is to be found in
the old definition of the great poet, the old and
eternal definition, formulated anew by Matthew
Arnold: "The great poet is he that makes the
most powerful application of *essential* ideas to
life; this *always under the laws of poetic beauty
and poetic truth.*"

A clear, steady outlook on the world, an eye
as sure to catch the gold of the star as the star
is to give it out to the darkness, — the gift of
the seer; sympathy, earnestness, desire swift
and strong, thrice admirable under perfect con-
trol, — the gift of temperament; melody, mar-
vellous melody, and harmony of utterance ;
illumination, the last far charm of art, the
occasional accent beyond the reach of art —
the gifts of voice, — all this must be found in
a great poet; it is all found in Tennyson.
This seems to us the fact to begin with in an
attempt to reach the secret of the laureate's
power.   From this starting-point we naturally
proceed on direct lines, and we are not likely
to be bogged in secondary questioning which
finds him neither an epic nor a dramatic poet ;
which finds he has spoken cautiously, perhaps
narrowly, on questions political and theologi-
cal ; has failed to prove himself in person or by
pen a graceful mover in society, or the hailest
of fellows well met; and which, for a culminat-

ing discovery, finds he has not risen to the sublimity of Mr. Swinburne's notion of woman.

"The best and bravest of my own contemporaries," says Froude, "determined to have done with insincerity, to find ground under their feet, to let the uncertain remain uncertain; but to learn how much, and what we could honestly regard as true, and believe and live by it. Tennyson became the voice of this feeling in poetry; Carlyle in what was called prose."

Let us attain to this notion of Tennyson's strength and valor, and we shall hardly stick fast in the quagmire of lesser findings.

The severely "classic" taste of Fitzgerald led him to decide that we have the heart of Tennyson in the volume of 1842. "In Memoriam" had to him the "air of being evolved by a poetical machine"; though, he did not omit to add, one of the "highest order." We understand by this that in so sustained a work there is wanting the impression of the inevitable; the inevitable as it is shown, for example,

in the matchless bugle song. The effect pro-
duced by a lyric that leaps forth, finished, all
aglow with the amazing radiance that is beyond
the reach of labor — true it is that this can-
not be produced by a long poem ; but, on
the other hand, neither can the lyric, however
spontaneous, however suggestive of the god,
evidence the sturdy staying-power justly recog-
nized as an important part of the great poet's
heritage.   If the "lyrical œstrus" of "Mari-
ana," of the "Lady of Shalott," is not to be
found in "In Memoriam" or in the "Idylls,"
neither is the lyrical œstrus of "L' Allegro," of
"Il Penseroso," to be found in "Paradise Lost,"
or in "Samson Agonistes."   In estimating the
genius of Tennyson, we need not, we should
not, occupy ourselves with his round sixty
years of singing ; still we can illy spare "The
Princess," we cannot spare "In Memoriam,"
and the "Idylls of the King." With "Becket,"
forceful as it is, with "Queen Mary," and
"Harold"; with the "Cup," and the "Falcon,"

and emphatically with the " Promise of May,"
the case is different: these we may fitzgerald
out of the count.

" Barons and bishops of our realm of England,
    After the nineteen winters of King Stephen —
    A reign which was no reign, when none could sit
    By his own hearth in peace; when murder common
    As nature's death, like Egypt's plague, had fill'd
    All things with blood; when every doorway blush'd,
    Dash'd red with that unhallow'd passover;
    When every baron ground his blade in blood;
    The household dough was kneaded up with blood;
    The mill-wheel turn'd in blood; the wholesome plow
    Lay rusting in the furrow's yellow weeds,
    Till famine dwarft the race — I came, your King!
    Nor dwelt alone, like a soft lord of the East,
    In mine own hall, and sucking thro' fools' ears
    The flatteries of corruption — went abroad
    Thro' all my counties, spied my people's ways;
    Yea, heard the churl against the baron — yea,
    And did him justice; sat in mine own courts
    Judging my judges, that had found a King
    Who ranged confusions, made the twilight day,
    And struck a shape from out the vague, and law
    From madness. And the event — our fallows till'd,
    Much corn, repeopled towns, a realm again."
                         Becket, Act I., Scene 3.

" Menœceus, thou hast eyes, and I can hear
    Too plainly what full tides of onset sap

Our seven high gates, and what a weight of war
Rides on those ringing axles! jingle of bits,
Shouts, arrows, tramp of the hornfooted horse
That grind the glebe to powder! Stony showers
Of that ear-stunning hail of Ares crash
Along the sounding walls.   Above, below,
Shock after shock, the song-built towers and gates
Reel, bruised and butted with the shuddering
War-thunder of iron rams; and from within
The city comes a murmur void of joy,
Lest she be taken captive — maidens, wives,
And mothers with their babblers of the dawn,
And oldest age in shadow from the night,
Falling about their shrines before their Gods,
And wailing 'Save us.' "

Tiresias.

Though the excellencies of these verses may
be beyond the reach of any other living English poet, we miss in them the revelation, the
mystic individuality, of the young bard that
sang "Morte d'Arthur," and, holding the line
of triumph, passed on to the maturity of "In
Memoriam," and to the perfect art of "Guinevere," a poem where strength and beauty move
together unobstructedly and with unbroken
step for the longest time recorded in the annals
of our language. Landor could rise to the

style of "Becket," yes, Beddoes could give us snatches of it, could in a short, dramatic flight, surpass it : —

> " The rest that build up the great hill of life,
> From the crutch-riding boy to his sweet mother,
> The deer-eyed girl, and the brown fellow of war,
> To the grey head and grandest sire of all
> That's half in heaven, — all these are forth to-night. "

"But "Morte d'Arthur," "Ulysses," "Titho-nus," "Guinevere," are — we were about to say it — as far from "·Becket " as " Becket " is from " Festus."

If we are to omit the "Promise of May," it is equally a duty to pass "Locksley Hall Sixty Years After " ; this, not because of the presence of any particular sentiment, but simply because of the absence of poetry. We deny the right of criticism to affirm that this piece of writing is a personal revelation ; by so doing the privilege of the poet is violated, and his province miserably nar-rowed. Neither of the " Locksley Halls " necessarily reveals more than the phrase and

accent of speech of the young or of the old
Tennyson.

Though, as Fitzgerald rightly said, we had
the heart of Tennyson in the work of the first
twenty years of his authorship, now that we
have the "Princess," "In Memoriam," and
the "Idylls," what is the proper attitude to
assume toward these grand amplifications, these
splendid supplements, possible to the increased
wisdom of years? Shall we begin rightly with
their twofold gift of wisdom and beauty by
opining that the poet is over-modest in asserting
that the great threnody does not solve the
mysteries of life; by deciding that the joints
show too plainly in the "Idylls," or that the
dénouement is ethically or æsthetically deficient?
This is to begin at the wrong end, at the little
end. Native sympathy, naked sight, will see
the death song as the gentlest yet manliest of
records; the brave, unbroken revery of grief;
the quiet quest of united heart and head,
endeavoring to fathom and voice their sorrow,

to find, as far as in us lies, a solution for, and a
stay against, torturing mystery, to find solace
for an ever-present, all but insupportable loss.
We shall come upon philosophy, great phil-
osophy, in these renewed breathings of
profoundly pathetic music, yet the philosopher
will not once displace the poet; and we shall
share in a complete victory of song where
sturdier bards, in the clash of thought and
voice, have come out with soiled plumes and
broken blades, ay, bleeding with mortal
wounds. This tallest poetic monument of
our time displays throughout, the unchallenged,
unshared characteristic of Tennyson. Sus-
tained as the effort is, close as the one high
theme is held to, the thing said once is not
to be said again; no cunning can better it.
Native sympathy, naked sight, will see in
this slow, patient growth of as many years as
Chatterton lived, a much fuller, more diversi-
fied and extensive flowering than that of
"Lycidas" or of "Adonais." There will be

found the rich report of long and solemn vigils,
of a close and protracted watch on nature and
on man; a report which, beyond the imposing
presentation of personal discoveries, sums the
discoveries of others, among whom are num-
bered the strongest intellects and best hearts of
our day. Full trust, lucid exposition — never
black analysis — courageous prophecy, — here
is a return to the old office of the poet; it is,
after all, not the mourner but the seer, the
teacher — the seer that sees so deeply and so
plainly, the teacher that teaches so sweetly
we are hardly conscious of being taught —
it is, after all, the seer, the teacher, that is
foremost in "In Memoriam." The great truths
of morals and religion are once more set up,
this time in the trying light of modern learn-
ing, and with the unobstructed subtilty of
modern art. Such being the view of "In
Memoriam," the "Idylls" will appear firstly
as of the shadowy, evasive substance of legend;
secondly, it will be seen that the far-off, elu-

sive material is subdued by consummate work-
manship to the use of the poetic art of to-day ;
setting forth once more, in a manner fresh as
admirable, valiant, struggling man and the
lovely rulers, right or wrong, of his for-
tunes.

Full trust, lucid exposition, courageous
prophecy, perfect art — surely after a wrestling
bout with the giant Browning, after the din of
Swinburne, it is difficult to speak temperately
of Tennyson. The moment we enter his
presence, we have escaped chaos, we are rid
of unprofitable labor, are no longer stunned by
the empty sounds of fury ; we have no blasting
to do to get at his meaning, we have no wish
to put him out as a general conflagration.
Once more in the Enchanted Land, we are
guests of the lord of it. As runs the story
of the "wise birds" in the records of the
red man, —

"The spirits of Sun-place have whispered him words";

he sings, we listen and are at rest. It is a great privilege in these forgetful, distrustful, and rebellious days, to meet again one of the good old order of the Sons of Song; large brained, large hearted, serious, self-contained, hopeful, clear and sweet of speech.

If Chaucer was the "first finder of our fair language," Tennyson is the last finder of it; and because of this, not less than because of his years, is to be numbered among the fathers of song. The initial tribute due him is, that, long as he has sung, he has never misapprehended nor forgotten his office. Wholly in sympathy, always in touch, with the rapid development of knowledge characterizing the period, the one singer found in the front rank of the marvellous march of science, while absorbing all and subduing it to continuous use, he has encroached on the province neither of the pulpit, of the platform, nor of the editorial chair; but, leaving to moralists and propagandists what is rightfully theirs, has

reverently kept the old poetry road. The
name Tennyson is at once a guaranty for pure
song, and a warning against every vicious
mixum compositum of literature; throughout
the laureate's work, poem by poem and line by
line, is heard a sovereign rebuke to the
effrontery of rattling, brassy poetastry and
husky mongrelism.

We hear, of late, hoarse apostate voices raised
to banish youth and beauty; but they will
hardly cry barren the double font, the twin-fed
spring whence issue all the rivers of song,
whence issues this last river of it, the long
golden flow of Tennysonian melody, for a half-
century singing up the commonplace to the
level of the rare, for a half-hundred years sing-
ing the monotonous days bright with ever-
changing radiance. Has Tennyson fallen short,
has he offended? He may be forgiven all, for
the sake of his allegiance to the beautiful, to
the good. All latter-day clamor to the con-
trary, the poet holds the old place; he is still

the servant of beauty. Each singer has his own way of serving; Tennyson has his way, as individual as it is faithful. Keats was truly the chosen darling of beauty; his wavy head was seldom raised from her breast, where it soon sank, pillowed forever. Tennyson, of a hardier nature, a man grown, beauty's lover, is a true son of the rugged race of man; who, if a familiar figure at gatherings of the gods, is there in the employ of the good mother ground. He goes but to return duly, bringing with him lavish gifts for our solace and delight. This poet has wings, still in his highest flight he soars no higher than the heart and head of humanity, mindful that, —

> . . . "the talk
> Man holds with week-day man in the hourly walk
> Of the mind's business, is the undoubted stalk
> True song doth grow on."

We have said that Tennyson may be pardoned many shortcomings for the sake of the bottom virtue of being first and last a poet. If,

poet of the ground, he is, unlike Shelley, poet
of the air; if he is unlike Keats, in that even
the realized fairyland of Greece cannot draw
him from the parent soil; if, unlike Words-
worth, he is always a poet, he has still fewer
points in common with the Georgian torrent,
the resistless misanthrope, who deemed his
habitual achievement an impossibility. "No
poetry," Byron writes Murray, "is *generally*
good — only by fits and starts — and you are
lucky to get a sparkle here and there." The
"sparkle" theory will work, last of all, in the
case of Tennyson. His is the steady glow be-
tokening the poet always a poet; and by this
constancy, this excess, of light, perhaps the
clearest-sighted of his readers — accustomed to
the heavy dappling of shadow in the region of
fit-and-start song — are not a little blinded. A
recent observer has registered a much wiser
saying than Byron's, applicable alike to the
work of the poet singly and to that of his
period : "Great excellence has from the begin-

ning of things been more uniform than medioc-
rity." Uniformity of great excellence — the
expression is pre-eminently pertinent to the
verse of our venerable representative of song
for the present time.

Nor is uniformity of excellence all; the uni-
formity is discoverable along many distinct,
widely diverging lines. When we consider
Tennyson, we must bear in mind not simply
inimitable lyrics, some of them unsurpassed in
any language; not simply magic landscapes
which so mate the mind and heart dwelling on
them that it were hard to say whether they
belong most to nature or to man, — the human
rippling of the "Brook Song," the human
honey-dropping of the "Talking Oak"; not
simply the exquisitely rich descriptions of "A
Dream of Fair Women," or of "The Palace
of Art"; not simply the profound passion
of "Love and Duty," or the burning words of
"Fatima"; not simply the exhaustive satire of
"Sea Dreams"; not simply the august dra-

matic power of "Morte d' Arthur," "Tithonus,"
"Ulysses," or "St. Simeon Stylites," these
vying in might and magnificence with the lines
of the blind Titan of the "Paradises"; not
simply the manly strength, the womanly loveli-
ness, the day and the night, the wondrous
round of the seasons, — the twofold passion of
earth and of the soul, borne to us in the wholly
new strains of the "Idylls"; not simply their
composite, epic picture of humanity in its
might and in its weakness, fragrant, permeated
with the very breath of nature, and quick with
her fervor, yet hung aloft in the upper realm
of art; not simply this, nor yet that long,
glorious toil up through the darkness of doubt
to the white height of hope and peace, — the
divinely isolated "In Memoriam"; — not sim-
ply one, but all of these and their high-born
kindred must we remember when we would
take the stature, not of the English lord,
but of the English poet, plain old Alfred
Tennyson.

For more years than span the average life of man his song has flowed, a full river of delight, nourishing on either bank nearly every variety of growth known to the inexhaustible soil of song. It were meet to pause and reflect upon the blessings that have come of this long, long summer of song. Poetry is not the only gainer by it, the sister arts have been great gainers; which means corresponding gain, immense benefit, accrued to the souls of men. To Tennyson more than to any other man of to-day we owe the atmosphere in which song and music, and painting and sculpture may live; an air congenial enough to the best interests of man to preserve among its treasures the steadily imperiled, the always assaulted sense of beauty.

Travel when and whither he may, this one poet, we say, keeps the old poetry road.

> " All nature widens upward; evermore
> The simpler essence lower lies.
> More complex is more perfect, owning more
> Discourse, more widely wise."

The poet is a teacher; but the teaching must not be that of the schoolmaster, flat didacticism, instruction laid down in "utter nakedness." A poet might well preserve these verses, but it was getting too far away from the excellent substance of poetry, from the flawless material that goes to the making of the "Palace of Art"; too far away from poetry, and too near this : —

> " How comes law to bear eluding ? Not because of impotence:
> Certain laws exist already which to hear means to obey;
> Therefore not without a purpose these man must, while those man may
> Keep and for the keeping, happy gain approval and reward." (" La Sasiaz.")

Habitually vital and interesting in matter, straightforward, chaste and beautiful in speech, —always a poet, and in many points a poet of the first rank, a master of

> " high and passionate thoughts
> To their own music chanted " —

this tells in outline the story of Tennyson's genius.

And which shall we call him, the poet's poet or the people's poet? Here we gain another glimpse into his individuality, his sweep of feeling, his elasticity of intellect, his power of accommodation. It were difficult to name another poet to be commended with like confidence to every inquirer, from the man of business to the visionary, from the shop-girl to the scholar, from the artisan to the artist. Again, a poet of nature, like Burns, he is equally a poet of art, like — whom?

> " The white mist, like a face-cloth to the face,
>   Clung to the dead earth, and the land was still."

In the union of art and nature, in the creation of an all-pervading, all-absorbing atmosphere, Tennyson yields to none; and, Milton and Coleridge excepted, we have had no other so emphatically a master of the music of words — words rich in meaning — since Shakespeare.

Stedman says of his music that it is passion itself; a statement to be profitably pondered by those of the opinion that passion is not among Tennyson's possessions. The faculty of musical utterance, as Coleridge observes, is not an attachment to the poet, but an integral part of the imagination. Coleridge thought in music when he wrote verse, Tennyson thinks in music. The music and the meaning in his lines are more than interwoven, they are interfused; and so perfect is the fusion that the voice

> " overtakes
> Far thought with music that it makes,"

and, attesting virtues but imperfectly expressed by the phrase, the Virgil of English verse, affirms the enchanter.

We are indebted to Tennyson, the poet, as we are to Matthew Arnold, the critic, for insistence on the eternal truth that poetry is one thing, and prose, the best of it, quite another. In suppressed lines of the laureate's written in boyhood, we may find a more open

proclamation of this than in many a line
mature poets permit to stand. The verses
in the "Juvenilia" about the dying lamb,
prove the young author to be of the distinct
race of poets: —

> " In a time
> Of which he wots not, run short pains
> Through his warm heart ; and then from whence
> He knows not, on his light there falls
> A shadow ; and his native slope
> Where he was wont to leap and climb
> Floats from his sick and filmèd eyes,
> And something in the darkness draws
> His forehead earthward, and he dies."

It is easy to perceive differences between such
poems as "At a Solemn Music," "Ode on a
Grecian Urn," "Three Years She Grew," "The
Forsaken Merman," Hunt's "Grasshopper and
Cricket," and Emerson's "Snow-Storm"; is it
less easy to perceive that they have certain es-
sential poetic elements in common, that they are
all begotten and born of the royal family of
song? Tennyson's work is one constant exhibi-
tion of this kinship; and it is here, in the very

beginning, that he divides ways with his most illustrious contemporary. Song is an inheritance, perhaps the most precious of our inheritances. It has come down to us in an unbroken line from the great seers of old; and it is Tennyson's fortune to stand in the direct line of transmission, to sing songs that are a legitimate development of the ancestral strains. Hence, while others, too, are abreast with the ideas of our time, he is more successful than another in the beautiful application of them to life ; his every verse, every word, being a double voice, —a protest against the unlawful and temporary in song, and a plea for the beautiful and abiding, for the flower, for the fragrance of thought and speech.

> "So from the root
> Springs lighter the green stalk; from thence the leaves
> More aery; last the bright consummate flower
> Spirits odorous breathes."

The bright consummate flower breathing odorous spirits — such is the ancestral song, such is each transmission of it, such is Tennyson's singing.

As a last word, let us go for poetry not to the critic, foreign or native born, but to the poets themselves. And when we come to Tennyson we shall emphasize, not his sensitiveness to the presence of law and order, but that strange, inexpressible quality found even in so small compositions as the lyrics of the "Princess"; the supernal something that insures what the vastest schoolmastership in verse has never compassed, — immortality. Let us go to the poems themselves. Then philosophy will be the last thing that we shall think of inquiring about, metaphysics the last thing that we shall dream of inquiring about. We shall not ask the poet's plant for a list of the ingredients from which it sucked up the life that we see in its graceful shape and lovely colors, that we smell in its delicate fragrance. We shall drink in with delighted eyes whatever crude philosophic material has helped the light and the

warm winds and the pure dews of inspiration
to nourish its perfect being; we shall do
this unconsciously and blissfully, nothing
in our minds and hearts but the beautiful
flower and the wondrous fragrance, the blos-
som and the breath of the deathless plant of
song.

VI

SIX MINUTES WITH SWINBURNE

VI

SIX MINUTES WITH SWINBURNE

AFTER speaking as we have of the superiority of the laureate's subject-matter and of his intellectual and emotional grasp of it, we found further that we must style him the greatest living master of words. In saying this we were not unmindful of the unique genius of the younger English singer to whom we are indebted for startling manifestations of the technics of his art. Our expression concerns words rich in meaning, words that voice inspiration, that are the tongue of profound poetic thought. Mastery of the diction befitting great poetry is not discoverable in numberless words, each word new to its fellow, or in ringing repetitions of a few favorite words.

The great poet is not prodigal, but sparing, of
speech; none but Shakespeare — and he, rarely
— dare sow with the whole sack. " Poetry
teaches," says Emerson, " the enormous force
of a few words, and in proportion to the inspi-
ration, checks loquacity. " Here is the place
to begin to take the measure of the author of
the masterly "Atalanta in Calydon." His fling
at Whitman and Tupper, that they merely "ac-
cumulate words, " is of the boomerang sort,
returning to fall too near the feet of the
redoubtable thrower. For, speaking strictly
and with great poetry as the standard, Swin-
burne's astonishing feats of rhythm are less
poetry than a kind — and necessarily an infe-
rior kind — of music. Too definite for music,
they are too indefinite for poetry; nor are
they so much human breath as wind blown
through an animate harp, — hot, waste-born
blasts, the heat of which, like the wind de-
scribed by Saadi, makes the marrow boil in
the bones.

An uncontrollable flow of words, we say, tells against inspiration, opposes poetry. Poetry turns on intellect, on luminous, searching thought. This first; again, as it strikes us, Swinburne's verse, as a whole, does not exhibit among its excellencies the choice of vital subjects, subjects that repay the patient gaze of the seer. Nor do we always find the more fruitful of the subjects selected well thought out; and when they are well thought out we are moved to say that the verbal execution is still disproportionate to both the theme and the ideas. Take, for example, the grandly sonorous "Ave atque Vale." Here the thought is appropriate and sufficient; while the music *per se* is worthy of the noblest subject-matter. The defect in this ode is, that the subject-matter being ignoble, the disproportion between the music and the thought defeats the effect aimed at, the high poetic effect, attained only by a nice balance of thought and expression.

"Now all strange hours and all strange loves are over,
Dreams and desires and sombre songs and sweet,
Hast thou found place at the great knees and feet
Of some pale Titan-woman like a lover,
Such as thy vision here solicited,
Under the shadow of her fair, vast head,
The deep division of prodigious breasts,
The solemn slope of mighty limbs asleep,
The weight of awful tresses that still keep
The savour and shade of old-world pine-forests
Where the wet hill-winds weep " ?

When the poet, wholly a poet, looks into Heaven he finds the lowest circle of it at least a few feet

"Above the howling senses' ebb and flow."

Imagine Tennyson rising to the realm of spirits only to plunge to this monstrously mundane, this "hyperbrobdingnagian business"!

The wondrous verbal cunning granted, it is a little strange that the subjective poverty of this dirge has not prevented eminent critics from mentioning it so favorably in connection with "Lycidas," with "Adonais," and with " Thyrsis." As one of our authorities in liter-

ature has said, " The poet's office is to be a
voice." Ay, but he does not stop there; a
voice lifting " to a purer ether and a wider
reach of view." Shortcoming in this particu-
lar is insufferable when the song essays the
life beyond.

We breathe " purer ether " here : —

> " There entertain him all the saints above,
>   In solemn troops, and sweet societies
>   That sing, and singing in their glory move,
>   And wipe the tears forever from his eyes."

There is purer ether here : —

> " That light whose smile kindles the universe,
>   That beauty in which all things work and move,
>   That benediction which the eclipsing curse
>   Of birth can quench not, that sustaining love
>   Which through the web of being blindly wove
>   By man and beast and earth and air and sea,
>   Burns bright or dim, as each are mirrors of
>   The fire for which all thirst; now beams on me,
>   Consuming the last clouds of cold mortality."

Though our feet keep the green English
fields in " Thyrsis," there, too, the spirit takes
an upper, a " happier air." On the wings of
these three threnodies we take a long flight

heavenward; the dirge for Baudelaire, with its marvellous melody and harmony, after all suffers us to get no higher than the twin sphericities of Her Script Prodigiousness. Indeed, it is less a flight upward than a dig downward: the atmosphere, the sights and sounds, are of the underground:—

" Some dim derision of mysterious laughter
 .   .   .   .
 And from pale mouths some cadence of dead sighs —
 These only, these the hearkening spirit hears,
 Sees only such things rise."

A strain from "In Memoriam," in comparison, seems wafted from the angelic choir:—

 " Thy voice is on the rolling air;
  I hear thee where the waters run;
  Thou standest in the rising sun,
  And in the setting thou art fair.
  .   .   .   .
  Far off thou art, but ever nigh;
  I have thee still, and I rejoice;
  I prosper, circled with thy voice;
 I shall not lose thee tho' I die."

But subject-matter and thought-power aside, considering Swinburne simply as an artist in

words, is he wholly masterful in technics ?
There is a good old rule that the highest art is
to conceal art. Will it be said that it is the
wont of the genius before us to do this? Will
it be affirmed that he can be read without the
attention being first, if not last, on the art,
open and persistently conspicuous? Will it
be declared possible for this poet to snatch a
grace beyond the reach of art? It seems to
us much safer to say that if he passes the
limits of the artistic it must be for the region
of the artificial : —

" O sleepless heart and sombre soul unsleeping

  .   .   .   .

Dreams and desires and sombre songs and sweet."

It is Swinburne's misfortune, both as an
artist and as a seer, to be too original. The
poet is a reporter, a translator, not the maker,
of life ; and with the matter of life we must
have the compliant manner. Swinburne gives
comparatively little of the matter, and surely
his is not the manner, of life. What he con-

temptuously terms Byron's "rhetoric" gives much more of both. Byron, at his best, produces by simple means great effects; Swinburne, at his best, surprises us with deftness in the use of technics, intricate as unsuspected. Says a critic whom Mr. Swinburne admires, "We do not ask from the poet linguistic feats, difficulties overcome. We expect to be delighted, entranced, even inspired, so that we also, his readers, feel for a time that we, too, are of the prophets." Swinburne's art, indisputable as it is, falls short of this high illusion.

VII

MUSIC, OR THE TONE POETRY

VII

MUSIC, OR THE TONE POETRY

Musaeus terms music "man's sweetest joy." With this sweetest joy the air of Greece was filled. At home and in the public place, toil and recreation alike were set to the measures of song, the old and the young together invoking the mystic might that made the trees and rocks thrill and wax nimble under the playing of Orpheus; the rhapsodist tuned his harp before beginning to recite Homer, and the tragic choruses of the later poets swept over the thousands assembled, in one long wave of stately melody. From Homer down, the Greek poets were musicians; indeed, the sacred nine were all singers, and the pagan heaven, like our own, is thronged with rejoicing choristers. The Greeks deified poetry, and with it they deified music; for these two were one: the old poetry was literally song, it was all sung. In the olden time the philosopher, the lawgiver — the Greek word for law means also song — the priest, the prophet, was a poet and a singer; setting his words to melody, he sang them, accompanying his voice with a musical instrument. But long before the rise of Athens and of Rome — always profiting by the example of Athens — we find the Egyptians and the Hebrews accepting music as a divine art, and paying it the highest honor. The Egyptians held it in reserve for the noblest use, protecting it by law from debasing innovations; while First Chronicles so blossoms with the glorious public demonstrations of the great poet and musician king, one is ready to believe the ark, mounted in a new cart, was being continuously driven from the house of Abinadab: —

"*And David and all Israel played before God with all their might, and with singing, and with*

*harps, and with psalteries, and with timbrels,
and with cymbals, and with trumpets.*"

The Psalms, again, are one mass of proof
that music and poetry, among the ancient
Hebrews, ministered to all the moods of those
"strong, excepted souls," that they were the
voice of their deep experience of life — deep
beyond all depths reached since, imperishable
in expression, on record forever. Music was
the national solace and delight. What pathos
in good old Barzillai's refusal to go up with the
singing king to Jerusalem : —

" *Can thy servant taste what I eat or what I
drink, can I hear any more the voice of the sing-
ing men and singing women ?* "

The same haunting accent stamps that last,
memorable chapter of Ecclesiastes, where the
desolation is consummated at the hour when
" *all the daughters of music shall be brought
low.*" And Jeremiah, when foxes hold the
once-glorious Hill of Zion, and the skies
of his people are black with famine, does

not forget, amid such calamities, the loss of
music : —

" *The elders have ceased from the gate, the
young men from their music.*"

Meagre though it may have been, of itself,
as compared with our own, we probably under-
rate the music of the cultured ancients. In
view of their intellectual and spiritual advance-
ment, of the variety of their instruments, of
the lofty character of the ceremonies to the aid
of which music was summoned, it must have
been, considered independently of poetry, no
despicable power. The effect of music and
poetry, with their accessories, combined as they
were, for example, in the odes and tragedies
of Greece, we know was prodigious; but music,
pure, simple — this, too, had its power. The
Spartans moved to the fight to the tune of the
flute, and Pericles and Socrates, no less than
the bewitching and not wholly blameless Lamia,
played it to enhance the passing of the quiet
hour.

The growth of music has been slow; it was the last plant of art to come into full flower. We are largely indebted to the poets for its advancement. To make a new hole in the flute, to add a string to the lyre, was once a perilous experiment. It required courage as well as skill and enthusiasm; for the innovation was often condemned, and the rash genius bidden to resume the old instrument and the old tune. Timotheus could not smite as he might please; the addition of four new strings was a sufficient cause for the interference of the Spartan Parliament. It spoke, and he was compelled to vent his thought and passion on the old seven strings. In that far-off year, 346 B. C., the wisdom then in power deemed that to enlarge the scale was to make music effeminate. It erred, but the mistake is only further testimony to the sacredness of the power struggling toward the noonday light of our time.

The details of this long struggle, the introduction of notation, of the time-table, of

printing; the successive improvements of in-
struments — for example, the step from the
dulcimer to the harpsichord, from the harpsi-
chord to the spinet, from the spinet to the
piano-forte; the labors of the Provençal poets,
of the monks of the Middle Ages, the con-
flicts of secular and sacred song; the com-
posers who, one after another, enlarged the
work of their predecessors, — all this we pass
with a glance.

Italy and Germany long had the lead, but
England was one day to enter the lists with
verve and vigor of her own. If it was at the
touch of Italian charm that Shakespeare's
songs and Milton's mask were set to delightful
music, before the days of Anglo-Italian art
there were English composers of noble masses
and matchless madrigals; and we do not forget
that it was with the thoroughly English Purcell,
born in 1658, that music began a series of
epochal victories unbroken to this day.

Early in the eighteenth century, we see,

standing side by side, two colossal composers,
two Saxons, established in majesty, — George
Friedrich Haendel and Johann Sebastian Bach.
Clear, bracing, sublime Haendel; inexhaustible
Bach, music flowing from his soul with the
grace and purity of the water-brooks — at last
the time has come when they begin to take
their just rank as men, as intellects, as august
mind and soul powers, two of the sovereign
few destined to sway the world. The work of
these stupendous geniuses, and that of their
contemporaries and successors, is our inherit-
ance. Have we a right notion of this work?

Rousseau defines music as the "art of com-
bining sounds in a manner agreeable to the
ear." This is one of the small definitions, the
like of which we have found barring the way to
a true estimate of poetry. To know music it
is necessary, as in the case of poetry, to return
to the old high notion. If the Egyptians, as
before noted, protected music by legal meas-
ures, the Greeks regarded it as of so great

importance to the individual and to the state that any deviation from the standard of propriety, whether in the chant or in the recitative of religious service, in the hymns to the gods or in the voluptuous songs of revel at the feasts of love and wine, was an unpardonable offence. The findings of the Greeks in the case of music are valuable, because, as on other lines of investigation, they strike to the root, fix elementary principles. The first step is to acknowledge the power of music : "Musical training is a more potent instrument than any other, because rhythm and harmony find their way into the secret places of the soul, on which they mightily fasten."

So Greece speaks to us in the voice of Plato, whose idea England's Addison simply repeats when he says, music can "manage all the man." It is well, if possible, to learn how this fastening, this managing, is brought about; but the first thing, the main thing, is to know that, by one method or another, it is accomplished.

With the Greeks, then, and with the profoundest students of life since the Greeks, let us know, for once and all, that in dealing with music we have to do with a power that shares with poetry the sovereignty among the mysterious forces of intellectual and spiritual life.

From Rousseau to Cousin is a long step. " The peculiar power of music," says Cousin, " is to open to the imagination a limitless career, to lend itself with astonishing faculty to all our moods. . . . It awakens more than other arts the sentiment of the infinite."

Here we begin to perceive something of the immense meaning and of the extended operation of music. " The special and peculiar sphere of music," says Hegel, " is sentiment, always with the understanding that this may be in the highest degree charged with intellectual vitality." These excellent words are especially valuable because of their acknowledgment of the intellectual element in music.

Great music not only may, but must, be charged
with sight, with mind.

Mr. Hamilton pauses, in the midst of delight-
ful writing on landscape painting, to give
additional testimony to the presence of the
intellectual element : —

"I am inclined to believe that the communi-
cative powers of musical sounds are habitually
underrated. They deserve passing allusion
here in connection with landscape painting,
because music, like landscape art, is not strictly
what is called an intellectual pursuit, and is
held in exceedingly low estimation by all who
are insensible to it. But may not these vague,
musical expressions of thought and feeling be
the only expression possible for *those* thoughts
and *those* feelings? I have often felt, whilst
listening to great music, that something was
thereby communicated to me which could not
reach me through any other channel. Literary
expression is, no doubt, more practical and posi-
tive; but are we quite sure that it is higher,

merely because it is more definite? The same
narrow spirit of classification which roughly
sets down landscape painting as unmeaning,
would put music below poetry; but the more
we understand it, the more embarrassing it
appears to settle its place. It may be that
music expresses aspirations that words cannot
express, and these aspirations may very possibly
be higher than those we utter verbally."

The reach of music toward the heart of
things is even longer than that of poetry; and
we may say of it more emphatically that it
seeks the spirit, busies itself with the infinite.

"Musical! How much lies in that! All
inmost things, we may say, are melodious;
naturally utter themselves in song. The mean-
ing of song goes deep. Who is there that, in
logical words, can express the effect music has
on us? A kind of inarticulate, unfathomable
speech, which leads us to the edge of the
infinite, and lets us for moments gaze into that!
. . . See deep enough, and you see musically;

the heart of Nature *being* everywhere music if you can only reach it."

Such is the voice of Carlyle, speaking as nobly of music as he has spoken of poetry. It is a breath from the clear upper air; the marshes of parlor amusement lie far below. We are on the high level held by the master spirits.

"Music," responds Thoreau, "is the sound of the universal laws promulgated. It is the only assured tone. There are in it such strains as far surpass any man's faith in the loftiness of his destiny." And still another voice is borne to us from the hill-top. It is Heine's: "Perhaps music is the last word of art."

Poetry baffles us at last; music eludes us at the very beginning of our pursuit. Music is more elementary than poetry; it is the mother beauty. Poetry borrows from music, while music is self-sufficient, asking no return. It outstrips poetry in swift, leaping suggestion, it makes a yet severer demand on the imagination. Music is the parent life, the ever-sounding

sea, out of which, from age to age, have risen
all the shapes of excelling and imperishable
utterance. Formless in one sense, in another
sense it is all form. Submit Chladni's glass
plates, strewn with sand, to musical vibrations,
and the sand takes symmetric figures. We may
be sure that behind the melody there is Nature's
gesture, made with nicest obedience to the laws
of grace. The place of music among the
beauties is peculiar, it is the beauty of move-
ment: music is motion. Aristotle bends his
thought to this point: "Why," he asks, "do
rhythms and melodies, which are composed of
sound, resemble the feelings; while this is not
the case with tastes, colors, or smells? Can it
be because they are motions, as actions are also
motions? Energy itself belongs to feeling, and
creates feeling. But tastes and colors do not
act in the same way."

Helmholtz, quoting Aristotle approvingly,
gives us a saying too important to be omitted:
"It [music] arrogates to itself, by right, the rep-

resentation of states of mind which the other arts can only indirectly touch." We find this testimony often repeated. Music speaks for that in us which, otherwise, would have little or no expression. Where poetry fails to utter the mind and heart of man, where it ceases to speak for and to these, there music makes a beginning; it is the last accent of aspiration. Hence, the vagueness of music, which is often termed a weakness, is really its strength; the indefiniteness is a necessity of the high message.

It may be well to dwell a moment on this point; for, if it be well taken, to music in the noblest exercise of its office, words are a burden, a weight upon its wings. Music and poetry may unite in the production of beautiful, of sublime work; but each has its own peculiar power, and is most effective in its sole strength, and within its own limits. Nature guards faithfully, jealously, the boundary lines of the arts; they cannot be blurred without loss, cannot be obliterated without failure. The genius of Wagner can work wonders, but no genius can transcend elementary laws. Because of his confusion of the arts, if for no other cause, Wagner could not sound the depth, could not soar to the height, familiar to the free but law-abiding Beethoven, the Shakespeare of the world of sound. The heart of Wagner's error is his opposition to nature: so far as concerns the highest results of art, the elements brought together are internecine. Because music expresses what poetry cannot, and poetry expresses what music cannot, is no reason why the two, serving together, should double the power of utterance. The circles of these two arts are not coincident. The circle of poetry is the smaller, it lies within the circle of music; and not till music passes beyond the domain of poetry does it come to its own. We are greatly indebted to Wagner, but our debt to him does not efface the fact that the distinct forms of expression that he strove to unite in one grand whole do not unite, cannot unite, in the per-

fection possible to either form in the exercise of
its own sole energy. The line between prose
and poetry is fixed and ineffaceable; the line
between poetry and music is fixed and inefface-
able; the line dividing each art from the art
nearest it is fixed and ineffaceable. If all be
uncertain farther on, thus far, at least, we may
make sure. As for the world, so for the arts,
the golden compasses have swung through the
vast profundity, and the Voice has said:—

> " Thus far extend, thus far thy bounds,
> This be thy just circumference."

Heine is right: music is in itself a revelation.
This voice to the spirit is serious and truthful.
We have made bold to affirm elsewhere that
the first aim of great poetry is truth; the same
must be affirmed of great music. " I take
music in a very serious light," says the pure
Mendelssohn, " and I consider it quite inadmiss-
ible to compose anything I do not thoroughly
feel. It is as if I were to utter a falsehood:

for notes have as distinct a meaning as words, perhaps even a more definite sense." Music, like poetry, rests finally on truth. Haydn, with his simple, child-like trust, wrote always in remembrance of his God. At the head of the first page he penned *In nomine Domini;* at the end of the work, *Laus Deo.* Music, like poetry, rests finally on God. Consequently we find the noblest minds and hearts of history leaning on these two arts, twin-born in divinity. The heart and intellect of all in our knowledge, the man of sorrows, about to go out with his chosen twelve on that agonizing errand into the silent hills, first clad himself in the strength of song. Of all the testimony to the power of music and poetry, this record is the most pregnant and precious: "*And when they had sung an hymn they went out into the Mount of Olives.*"

The thinkers and tellers, the reporters, the masters of ideas and of expression, who furnish and fix in beauty nearly all the truths for

a hundred, perhaps a thousand, years, those
destined to completeness, to the maturity of
which man is capable, but rarely reaches, — the
Solomons, the Platos, the Shakespeares, the
Beethovens, — recognize the high, first powers
that govern them and their fellows, they
homage music.   Whither we turn, to whatever
clime or race of yesterday or of to-day, the
souls we know and love best we find knowing
and loving music.   These find it a source of
perpetual power, a font of life.   Where were
the Reformation without the man so filled with
music that for one of his hymns Frederick the
Great could find no smaller name than " God
Almighty's   Grenadier   March " ?   " Luther's
music," says Carlyle, " is heard daily in our
churches. . . . The great Reformer's love of
music, of poetry, it has often been remarked,
is one of the most significant features in his
character.   He it was, emphatically, who stood
based on the spiritual world of man, and only
by the footing and miraculous power he had

obtained there, could he work such changes in the material world."

The leading minds and souls — it cannot be too often repeated — lean upon poetry and music, and their tributes to these arts are of vastly greater importance to us than the discussion of technical details.

Hear Heine once more, as he recalls the · impression made on him by the playing of Paganini: ."There was not one ray of hope or consolation in the bottomless depths of those tones. When the saints of Heaven hear such sounds, the praises of God die on their lips, and weeping, they hide their pious heads."

The question is less what does music mean, than what may music not mean to the ear attuned? Jean Paul Richter, warning music off with frantic gesture, utters the wild cry, "Away! Away! Thou tellest me of things that I have not known in all this life, and shall never know!" It is of music that Milton speaks when he says: —

> " I was all ear,
> And took in strains that might create a soul
> Under the ribs of death."

Milton, like Luther, was more than a lover of music, he was a musician. In his verse the musician is wont to move step by step with the poet. "At a Solemn Music" is a river of harmony, of itself justifying the title, "Organ Voice of England."

> " Where the bright seraphim in burning row
> Their loud, uplifted trumpets blow,
> And the cherubic host in thousand choirs
> Touch their immortal harps of golden wires " —

when will the music of words rise to nobler strains? Browning finds in music "earnest of a heaven"; Coleridge finds in it one of the strongest arguments for immortality. Music lifts us into the clear, upper air, toward the high dwelling-place. Jean Ingelow has some beautiful lines on its descent from the upper home: —

" We know they music made
In heaven, ere man's creation;
But when God threw it down to us that strayed,
It dropt with lamentation,
And ever since it doth its sweetness shade
With sighs for its first station."

"Music is all said to be the speech of angels," speaks Carlyle; "in fact, nothing among the utterances allowed to man is felt to be so divine." The greater, the more original — that is, the more receptive — the intellect, the richer is the tribute to music. Let Cardinal Newman bear witness: " Take another instance of an outward and earthly form or economy under which great wonders unknown seem to be typified; I mean musical sounds, as they are exhibited most perfectly in instrumental harmony. There are seven notes in the scale; make them fourteen; yet what a slender outfit for so vast an enterprise! What science brings so much out of so little? Out of what poor elements does some master create his new world!"

Intellect, be it observed, must go to creation, to the creation of a "new world." Only metaphysics has an excuse for not seeing a truth plain as that in Hegel's saying, "Intellect and emotion are two inseparable elements of spirit"; and yet the hard judgment, the wisdom, underlying the emotion in great music is often not so much as suspected. The sympathetic, straight-seeing student finds it out. "No man," says one of George Eliot's characters, "has too much talent to be a musician. Most men have too little. ... We [the musicians] help to rule the nations, and make the age as much as any other public men. We count ourselves on level benches with legislators." Stronger yet is the language of George Sand: "Music expresses all that the mind dreams and foresees of mystery and grandeur. It is the manifestation of a higher order of ideas and sentiments than any to which human speech can give expression. It is the revelation of the infinite."

Such testimony must give us the case, soon or late; one day we shall be rid of the emotion fallacy both in music and in poetry. Because some gifted child composes meritorious sonatas, at six years of age; because a Blind Tom renders, after a fashion, compositions of the masters; because an idiot whistles tunes correctly, the vanity of a certain kind of intellect is not to look down on music, is not to ascribe it wholly to the emotions. Women exhibit a richer, a finer, development of the emotional nature; where are the female composers? To glance at Beethoven's face is to see that he is a strong *man*, one of the giants of mind. Brain, the creative power, fairly stares from it. It is the face of one that has confronted life in all its aspects, the face of one before whose steady gaze the darkness of mystery is shot through with rays of eternal day. Beethoven's face is an index of the only mind among the moderns, unless it be Michael Angelo's, that we mate with the mind of Shakespeare; it is the face of

one that could record life in the purest, the most
exacting and imaginative language known to
man. As the days go on, fewer and fewer will
affirm that there is more of life, of the human
soul, and all that is essential to it, in "Hamlet"
than in the "Ninth Symphony." Where the
words of the poet cease, the tones of the musi-
cian begin to sound, and the wondrous circle of
life, of knowledge, of love and hope, is closed.
To make these two masters our own is worth
all the effort required; and it is immense. In-
deed, effort, unaided, can never accomplish this;
we must be, in a measure, word poets and tone
poets ourselves. Beethoven was from youth an
enthusiastic student of Shakespeare. "How
shall I set to work to compose?" young Wag-
ner asks Beethoven. "Read Shakespeare,"
is the answer. Shakespeare has his rightful
place, Beethoven is yet to take his. The few
know him as he is; when he comes to be so
known by the many, it will be an era in culture.
"So that genius exists," runs a saying of Schu-

bert, " it matters little how it appears, whether
in the depths, as with Bach ; on the heights, as
with Mozart; or in the depths and on the
heights at once, as with Beethoven." From
the depths to the heights — that is the range
of Beethoven. Schubert speaks of Beethoven
as we do of Shakespeare. He knows the speech
of music, he has sat lovingly at the feet of the
greatest master of that language.

A cultured critic, speaking of the scherzo
movement of Beethoven's "Seventh Symphony,"
says, "No language can explain the depth of
thought enshrined in those awful notes sus-
tained by the horns in that wonderful episode
in D Major." The words are "depth of
thought." One that knows Beethoven knows
intellect, intellect in one of its most astounding
phases. When that opulent and impudent
brother sent up his card to the poor musi-
cian — " Beethoven, Land-owner," what was
scrawled on the back of it before it was re-

turned? Emotion-owner? No; "Beethoven, Brain-owner."

It is our wont to think of the musician merely as one skilled in some particular line of the art's development. With the great musician we cannot stop there; we must go on, as did the servants of Saul in their report of the royal poet and musician. Not only is he "*cunning in playing*," but also a "*mighty, valiant man, and a man of war, and prudent in matters, and a comely person.*" Nor is the description finished yet: "*and the Lord is with him.*" Assuredly, if the Lord is with any that cling their little time to our whirling world, He is with the great seers of life, the poets and the musicians; and if we are to know life, it is to these seers we must turn. Culture, full life — this it is we seek. It can never be obtained till we add to the revelations of the Hebrew and the Greek poets, of Dante, of Shakespeare and Milton, the revelations of their compeers, Bach, Haendel, and Beethoven. If it is well to remem-

ber that the shapes of "Paradise Lost" rose
before the sightless eyes of Milton, it is equally
well to remember that the strains of the "Nine
Symphonies" surged, a sea, in the deaf ears of
Beethoven. Shakespeare opened a new world;
Beethoven opened a newer and more startling
world. After all the leading up to them, the
symphonies were a revelation. We shall not
have the last revelation of life, — to say it once
more — until we know the poets, the seers; but
we must know both the word poets and the
tone poets, both the seers of speech and the
seers of pure sound.

The wisdom of the world, both ancient and
modern, attests the value of music as a means
of culture. Milton in his exordium to youth
bids them be familiar with the "solemn and
divine harmonies of music, . . . which, if wise
men and prophets be not extremely out, have
a great power over dispositions and manners,
to smooth and make them gentle from rustic
harshness and distempered passions." In the

"Spirit of Laws" we find a fuller statement. "That judicious writer, Polybius," says Montesquieu, "informs us that music was necessary to soften the manners of the Arcadians, who lived in a cold, gloomy country; that the inhabitants of Cynaetha, who slighted music, were the cruelest of all the Greeks, and that no other town was so immersed in luxury and debauch. Plato is not afraid to affirm that there is no possibility of making a change in music without altering the frame of government. Aristotle, who seems to have written his politics only in order to contradict Plato, agrees with him, notwithstanding, in regard to the power and influence of music over the manners of the people. This was also the opinion of Theophrastus, of Plutarch (Life of Pelopidas), and of all the ancients; an opinion grounded on mature reflection, being one of the principles of their polity." History silences all question concerning the power of music as a lever to better living. Matthew

Arnold, while so earnestly urging us upward to a higher life, should have put music with poetry as a mighty helper. He should have bade these go hand in hand as of old; for much of the "best that has been thought and said in the world" is to be found in the tone poetry.

Lovers of music associate its power with the future; it points them to high estates, to rich possessions, somewhere in waiting. The future and infinity — of these music speaks as by a native necessity, by a special and sovereign prerogative. Music inspires hope, pictures the splendors of immortality. But the reach of music into the future is hardly more characteristic than its peculiar haunting of the past. "It recalls," says Coleridge, "the deep emotions of the past with an intellectual sense of proportion." — Here, also, we are not left in doubt as to the intellectual in music. — George Eliot felt strongly the power of music over the past. . . . "To feel," she says, "its won-

drous harmonies searching the subtlest wind-
ings of your soul, the delicate fibres of life
where no memory can penetrate, and binding
together your whole being, past and present,
in an unspeakable vibration." Jean Paul states
the power of music over the past and the future
in a single sentence: "When I hear music, it
is as if I heard a loud past or a loud future."
The pathos of poetry often finds its nearest
perfect expression in a call to the past; it is
so with music. Music identifies itself with a
person, place, or experience with all the sub-
tilty of an odor. No power can more vividly
recall a vanished form or face. Chaucer's
lover bears witness to this: —

> " And if he hearde song or instrument,
>   Then would he weepe."

Music is universal in its ministry; rare is the
time, place, or condition that it may not serve.
There are individuals without music; but we
have no record of a nation destitute of it. An
old voyager says of the Sagaleen Islanders,

"They can all educe pleasing sounds from a large stalk of celery, or a species of euphorbium, open at both ends. They blow into the smaller end, and the sound does not badly resemble the soft tones of the trumpet." All nations have music; and while it has been, and is, to a greater or less degree characteristic, it is destined to become more and more, as the art advances, a test of the temper of the people giving it birth, a decisive factor of national life. Confucius, a century before Plato, said, "Wouldst thou know if a people be well governed, if its manners be good or bad, examine the music it practises."

We need not fear lest we exaggerate the importance of music; it is the heart's bread. How sweet the help to wear away the long days

> "When on the knap of yonder hill,
> The shepherd tunes his quill"!

The quill is tuned on the grassy height, while within doors

> " All at her work the village maiden sings,
>   Nor while she turns the giddy wheel around,
>   Revolves the sad vicissitudes of things."

If Ovid's miner is singing his untaught music amid the clanking of his chains, the sailor is trolling his wild song in mid-ocean: wherever toil is, there, too, is music.

But, while finding that music is not only the friendliest, but, at its highest, the purest of arts, of the powers that hold sway over heart and mind, can we go so far as to find, with Jean Paul, that it is unable to express the impure? On the contrary, if we bear in mind that music is the most direct expression of desire, that it is emphatically the voice of our inmost secrets, that it may utter pleasingly thoughts and feelings that would offend, even shock, us if couched in the cruder form of words, we shall be more likely to conclude that its strength may be as dangerous when perverted as it is beneficent when rightly employed. The powers have a white and a black side. As far back as the

days of Amos, we find music inveighed against
as the accessory in iniquity of them that "*lie
upon beds of ivory, and stretch themselves upon
their couches, and eat the lambs out of the flock,
and the calves out of the midst of the stall; . . .
that drink wine in bowls, and anoint themselves
with the chief ointments.*"   Here, plainly enough,
music is the companion of sloth, gluttony, and
all the tribe of debauch.   There is a severe
Talmudic saying that serves in this connection:
"The ear that often listens to music shall be
rooted out."   And Plato has a pertinent word:
"Damon will tell you what sounds are capable
of corrupting the mind with base sentiments,
or of inspiring the contrary virtues."   He
says further, that the Egyptians permitted only
certain moral music to reach the ears of the
young.   When the Trojan lover declines to
battle with Menelaus, Hector scoffs at

> "His graceful form, instilling soft desire,
> His curling tresses and his sylvan lyre."

And there is no mistaking the drift of Gloster's "lascivious pleasing of the lute." The lute as touched in the lady's chamber, and the "low, voluptuous music" winding through the "Palace of Sin," tell us that Jean Paul and Montesquieu go too far when they affirm that music cannot express the impure, that it is the only art that does not corrupt the mind.

Much has been said, old and new, of the power of music over disease. Pythagoras recommends it for mental disorders, while Thales is said by means of it to have stayed the ravages of a pestilence at Sparta. Undoubtedly music is remedial in cases of nervous affection, is medicinal to unquiet minds. In a runic chapter of "Hava-mal," music and poetry combine to produce a panacea: "I am possessed of songs; such as neither the spouse of a king, nor any son of man can repeat; one of them is called the Helper: it will help thee at thy need, in sickness, grief, and all adversities."

> " Grief who need fear
> That hath an ear ? "

asks a sixteenth century poet ; and Shakespeare,
as always, comes to the heart of the matter at
a stroke : —

> " In music is such art,
> Killing care and grief of heart."

Nor does the influence of music stop with
man. The lines beginning,

> "For do but note a wild and wanton herd,"

are a masterly exhibition of its control over the
creatures beneath him.

Given music's power over manners and mor-
als, its influence in religion is obvious. There
is serious truth in Dr. Holmes's

> " Not all the preaching, O my friend,
> Comes from the church's pulpit end."

Milton tells us what church music should be
—a thing, unfortunately, very different from
what it is —

> . . . " With sweetness through mine ear
> Dissolve me into ecstasies,
> And bring all heav'n before mine eyes."

It is too true that we no longer take either music or poetry for what they are. The old notion has well nigh faded out. Pythagoras deemed it a wise expenditure of his time to advance the art by careful research, Aristotle to dwell on its power over morals, Plato to explain its use as a means of bringing man into harmony with himself and his surroundings; our wise men, our philosophers, think best to busy themselves with other things. Were it not better in the matter of music, as in the matter of poetry, to return to the old notion, to hold dear the companionship of this most friendly, this beneficent and unfailing power? Reflect, for a moment, how closely it is interwoven with every fibre of life. Music has attended the world from its birth: it is an inheritance of the elements, a gift to all living things, rising higher and higher till it moves the mind and heart, and shapes the expression, of immortal man. Carlyle is right: the heart of nature truly is music. Touch her, move her, anywhere, and the response is melody. The singing of the Egyptian sands is typical of nature throughout: all is music, all is song. It was a profound imagining of Pythagoras, that music of the spheres. Soon as man listened he heard a voice, and felt that it reached so far beyond the human limit that perchance the roving stars might catch it, to repeat upon their shining round. This is too beautiful, too true, an imagining for the great poets to overlook. We come upon it again in "Paradiso," again in the Christmas ode, —

> "Ring out ye crystal spheres,"

and once more as an ornament of the one perfect love poem of the world: —

> "There's not the smallest orb which thou beholdest
> But in his motion like an angel sings,
> Still quiring to the young-eyed cherubims."

Shakespeare knew the power of music. Only music itself can surpass the strength and delicacy of his words concerning it. No other

poetry comes so near as Shakespeare's to slipping
back from articulation into the mother sound : —

> " That strain again! it had a dying fall:
> Oh, it came o'er my ear like the sweet south,
> That breathes upon a bank of violets,
> Stealing and giving odour ! "

The "Tempest" is one superb verbal sym-
phony. Soft, viewless viols of love lure Fer-
dinand to Miranda's bower : —

> " Where should this music be ? I' th' air or th' earth ?
> It sounds no more; and sure, it waits upon
> Some god o' th' island."

Sweet breathings, as from the realm of sleep,
enchant even savage Caliban; while stern voices
of the grand chorus hymning forever the good
and beautiful, stun the guilty soul of King
Alonso : —

> " Methought the billows spoke, and told me of it,
> The winds did sing it to me; and the thunder,
> That deep and dreadful organ-pipe, pronounc'd
> The name of Prosper: it did base my trespass."

Next after the golden cadence of Milton, in
its tribute to the music of nature, we may place

that subtilest passage of Wordsworth, where the
beauty of natural music passes into the very
being of the lovely listener, and becomes visible
in her features : —

> " The stars of midnight shall be dear
> To her; and she shall lean her ear
> In many a secret place
> Where rivulets dance their wayward round,
> And beauty born of murmuring sound
> Shall pass into her face."

Yes, nature is all music; earth, sea, and air
sing their numberless songs and play their
myriad instruments forever; but it is in the
eternal soul of man that are to be heard the
ravishing melodies, the divine harmonies.   The
man shut out from these stands amid deplorable
desolation.   Dismal, indeed, is his inheritance,
a heart "dark as Erebus."   Shakespeare can
pronounce the curse on him whose ears are
closed; for the blessing on him that has ears
to hear, even Shakespeare has no language.

VIII

HAWTHORNE

VIII

HAWTHORNE

I

THOUGH in strictness Hawthorne is not to be numbered among the poets, we shall go rather right than wrong if we take him at the word of the author of the "Vision of Sir Launfal": "He was certainly the greatest poet, though he wrote in prose, . . . that America has given to the world." And since Mr. James's study of Hawthorne has been deemed, on the whole, a commendable survey of our great romancer's genius, the more convenient, and perhaps the more profitable, way to express our view of Hawthorne, and at the same time to touch once more on what we

257

conceive to be the right lines of criticism, is to begin with a little scrutiny into Mr. James's qualification for his task, and a brief consideration of his method in the prosecution of it.

If there is any one quality requisite for a critic, it is sympathy with his subject, and we should hardly look first to Mr. James as the man most likely to be alive with sympathy for Hawthorne. Hawthorne stands for idealism, imagination, and, Mr. James would add, for the American spirit; while Mr. James is a realist, born and bred, a citizen of the world withal, wont to delight in girding at the land that gave him birth.

Disqualification is suggested at the very start; the opening page of this contribution to the " English Men of Letters " series betrays a suspicious loftiness: " His [Hawthorne's] works consist of four novels, and the fragment of another, five volumes of short tales, a collection of sketches, and a couple of story-books for children ; and yet some account of the man and

the writer is well worth giving." Quantity, of
course, may become a factor of an author's title
to remembrance; where, however, the quality
is as fine, as choice, as it is in Hawthorne, a
model cosmopolitan might find a better way of
apprising us of the fulness of his resources
than by instituting a search for it at the
outset. Had only four little volumes of Haw-
thorne been found, — the "Scarlet Letter,"
"Mosses from an Old Manse," the "Blithedale
Romance," and a volume of the short tales,
— probably Mr. James's Hawthorne would
never have been born; but, finally, having
found the chary romancer worth writing about,
he proceeds, on the regulation line of the later
scientists, to deplore his environment. "If,"
he says, "there is something very fortunate
for him in the way that he borrows an added
relief from the absence of competitors in his
own line, and from the general flatness of the
literary field that surrounds him, there is,
also, to a spectator, something almost touching

in his situation." Starting from the "almost
touching" point, our realistic critic is very
successful in following up the environment;
so successful, indeed, that the figure environed
is well nigh lost sight of. "We are struck,"
he continues, "with the large number of ele-
ments that were absent from them [his circum-
stances], and the coldness, the thinness, the
blankness . . . present themselves so vividly
that our foremost feeling is that of compassion
for a romancer looking for subjects in such a
field." Then follows a list of things missing,
the schedule finally closing after the true
Anglican manner: "No great universities, nor
public schools, — no Oxford, nor Eton, nor
Harrow; no literature, no novels, no museums,
no pictures, no political society, no sporting
class — no Epsom nor Ascott."

Who is really the misser, the mourner, here?
We feel that it is not so much Hawthorne as
Mr. James. Hawthorne may mention some of
these missing things, but it is left for Mr.

James to lay stress upon them, and that not always with the accent of the true critic: "The natural remark in the almost [not "touching," this time, but "lurid"] lurid light of such an indictment would be that, if these things are left out, everything is left out. The American knows that a good deal remains; what it is that remains — that is his secret, his joke, as one may say. It would be cruel in this terrible denudation, to deny him the consolation of his natural gift, that 'American humor' of which of late years we have heard so much."

If sympathy with his subject is one of the first requisites for the critic, hardly second comes a proper attitude toward all subjects, — a patient, impartial spirit, a right temper.

"Hawthorne," says Mr. James, "was in his disposition an unqualified and unflinching American; he found occasion to give us the measure of the fact during the seven years that he spent in Europe towards the close of his life; and this was no more than proper on

the part of a man who had enjoyed the honor
of coming into the world on the day on which,
of all the days in the year, the great Republic
enjoys her acutest fit of self-consciousness.

.   .   .   .

"This seems to me to express very well the
weak side of Hawthorne's work — his constant
mistrust and suspicion of the society that sur-
rounded him, his exaggerated, painful, morbid,
national consciousness.   It is, I think, an indis-
putable fact, that Americans are, as Americans,
the most self-conscious people in the world, and
the most addicted to the belief that the other
nations of the earth are in a conspiracy to
undervalue them.   They are conscious of being
the youngest of the great nations, of not being
of the European family, of being placed on the
circumference of the circle of civilization rather
than at the centre, of the experimental element
not having as yet entirely dropped out of their
great political undertaking.   The sense of this
relativity, in a word, replaces that quiet and

comfortable sense of the absolute, as regards
its own position in the world, which reigns
supreme in the British and in the Gallic
genius."

Such passages as these — and they are of the
pervading atmosphere of the volume — we think
aside from the true purpose, off the right line
of criticism. The writing of them is something
worse, indeed, than pressing minor points; it
is impertinence. Mr. James's avowed purpose
is rather criticism than biography, and he is so
nice in the matter that the tone of Mr. Lath-
rop's biography·fails to please him: "his tone,"
he says, "is not to my mind the truly critical
one." Unmistakably, the goal is true criticism;
but were it reached, there would be no occasion
to observe that the Hawthorne that is, and will
be· remembered, is not the Hawthorne of the
"English Notes," nor could we get the impres-
sion that so much room is given the "Notes"
less as a means of interpreting Hawthorne's
genius than as a field wherein may be exer-

cised a certain serene, cosmopolitan, polished causticity.

Hawthorne's "exteriority" in English society admitted, we have done little toward ravelling the imagination that produced the "Scarlet Letter." The sympathetic, serious critic does not trouble himself over Ascotts and Epsoms and exteriorities, he escapes the fate of miring in the environment. Nothing can be clearer than that it is merely as a background to give his personified forces of the universal mind and heart body and lodgment that Hawthorne uses his own people and the soil from which he sprang. Provinciality is not at the core; it is the setting for phenomena of life elementarily identical in all times and in all places.

"American intellectual standards are vague, and Hawthorne's countrymen [Hawthorne's countrymen, not Mr. James's own] are apt to hold the scales with a rather uncertain hand and a somewhat agitated conscience"; nevertheless, we are constrained to say, that there

are those among us with culture and skill
enough, not only to distinguish Mr. James's
Hawthorne from the original but, to perceive
that constitutional differences between the
critic and the romancer make the critic more
at ease in deviations from his theme. Haw-
thorne's "Journal," for example, is in the
direct way of his work, and is a standing puzzle
to him. "Outward objects," he says, "play
much the larger part in it; opinions, convic-
tions, ideas pure and simple are almost absent."
On failure to discover a better *raison d'être* for
the day-book, the note-book, than mere exer-
cise, a morning jog round the writer's course
to keep in training, Mr. James could have
profited by conference with a fellow-country-
man, no other than the son of Nathaniel Haw-
thorne.

"Hawthorne endeavors," says the son, "to
balance his rare faculty of insight by the com-
paratively common faculty of out-sight; and
the volumes of his note-books are the patent

records of this study." When one recalls the minute detail with which it is often Hawthorne's pleasure to picture a scene (for example, the old Pyncheon garden when Phœbe trips out into it on the first morning of her visit), the purpose of the dry catalogue of natural appearances becomes unmistakable. The bare items before the writer, his ever-ready imagination adorns them and groups them in a picture of singular beauty, giving to his airy concepts substance and verisimilitude.

Plainly, cosmopolitan tendencies and linguistic skill are not, of themselves, effectual for criticism. Our experienced guide is, after all, unfamiliar with the way, even to the degree of never having discovered the innate impulse, the push of nature, in the born writer that forces him into authorship despite a thousand obstacles. If we mis-read him on this point, certain it is that he so far fails to comprehend Hawthorne as to number him among the artisans of letters, who coolly weigh the pain and pleas-

ure, the gain and loss of authorship with that of
any business or trade. "It strikes the observer
to-day," he says, "that Hawthorne showed
great courage in entering a field in which the
honors and emoluments were so scanty as the
profits of authorship must have been at that
time." Shortsighted, belittling as this comment
is, for one-half the reward — the "honors" —
it contradicts a gratuitous statement closely
preceding: "If the tone of the American world
is in some respects provincial, it is in none
more so than in this matter of the exaggerated
homage rendered to authorship. . . . There
is no reason to suppose that this was less the
case fifty years ago."

Again, if Hawthorne's environment, bald as
Galba's head, his *ne plus ultra* of provinciality
and his pitiful exteriority among Britons,
trouble Mr. James, his transcendental tenden-
cies positively shock him. We had thought no
sensibilities too fine for a portrayal of Haw-
thorne; but, really, one unable to look without

a shudder on the every-day Thoreau out on a cross-lot stroll, is not the chosen reporter of the owly flights in which our Yankee enchanter so delighted.

But, perhaps we have gone far enough to indicate our reasons for finding that nature seems not to have equipped Mr. James for just the task in hand, that he moves "rather in a maze than in a way." After all, he is at times so close on the right line of criticism and always so crafty in word-handling, one cannot find fault with a will. We wish we might remember only the right and important things so admirably said, that it were not a duty to bear in mind also the wrong and trivial things set down with the same well-bred solicitude. We wish it were possible to wave off an alien, if graceful, shape posed between us and Hawthorne, an airy nothing, yet with substance enough to bewhisper us, "I serve Sir Censor to the Thames."

II

Now, turning from the " thin New Englander
with a miasmatic conscience," the abuser of the
" fanciful element " of a " certain superficial
symbolism," — turning from Mr. James's Haw-
thorne to the Hawthorne that was and is,
let us remember that, the shyest, most soli-
tary of men, he passed his youth mainly in the
company of nature, his own thought, and a
few books. Among the first read of the few
books were, we are told, the " Faerie Queene "
and " Pilgrim's Progress," which might well
strengthen his native bent toward allegory.
The lad was writing short stories in a random
way before he went to Bowdoin, at seventeen.
While Hawthorne may be called, to the last, a
desultory writer, he was a continuous brooder,
and such energy as he expended was always in
the direct line of his chosen work. Men that
the world calls idle are, often, very busy after
their own fashion. Hawthorne's was a long

and lonely vigil before the world found him out. When it did find him, it discovered no novice, but a ripe artist. His isolation and obscurity worked in the main to his advantage. He, himself, was thoroughly convinced of this. "And now," he says, "I begin to understand why I was imprisoned so many years in this lonely chamber, and why I could never break through the viewless bolts and bars; for if I had sooner made my escape into the world, I should have grown hard and rough, and been covered with earthly dust, and my heart might have become callous by rude encounters with the multitude. But living in solitude till the fulness of time was come, I still kept the dew of my youth, and the freshness of my heart." We rightly turn to age for counsel, to youth for action; but youth, too, has a wisdom of its own. "People always fancy that we must become old to become wise," says Goethe; "but, in truth, as years advance, it is hard to keep ourselves as wise as we were."—"Years and travel," he says again, "are not indispensable to the ripening of every mind. Knowledge of the world is inborn with the genuine poet. He needs not much or varied observation to represent it adequately. I wrote 'Götz von Berlichingen' at two and twenty."

Julian Hawthorne, who sees his illustrious father's purpose and achievements in a clear light, says his endeavor was "to investigate and analyze, without danger or confusion, the problems and perplexities of the human heart." We would add to this, *for the use of the artist:* to investigate heart problems for the use of the artist. This is included in the aim of the novelist; it is by his method that Hawthorne is set at a distance from the novelist. His method is rather that of the poet; he symbolizes heart problems instead of presenting actual personages. This method, applied to the peculiar themes selected, resulting often in a somewhat chilling mist and intangibleness, as of ghosts, demands so much imagination from

the reader, and appeals so lightly to the
affections, that he can never be, in the wide
sense, popular.   His is the realm of personified
abstractions, these often touched in by a few
delicate lines ; and it is not every one that can
follow him as he summons forth and reviews
the dim, impalpable shapes that come and go at
his command.   Were these abstractions of the
lighter, of the surface, phenomena of the heart,
Hawthorne's airy visitors would be easier to
fellowship with ; but we should then be under
the "spell," — begging Mr. James's pardon, —
the "spell" of a mere necromancer, instead of
subjects of a kingly imagination, daring, strong,
as it is subtile and restrained.   Hawthorne
was imagination in the flesh.   Imagination and
fancy load his most fragile theme ; and to strip
them away would be to leave a skeleton one
would hardly deem it possible to so build on
and vivify as to make it a thing of beauty.
Here is Hawthorne's skill and charm ; and,
conscious of it, he was perpetually adding to

the number of the meagre, hard-outlined notes of natural appearances, — so distressing, baffling, to Mr. James, — by cunning use of which he held warp and weft of gossamer to the ground. Had Hawthorne employed fancy only, he would have left an enviable reputation; as it is, the employ of it seems to have been frequently the indulgence of a native bent as a means of rest from the exhausting exercise of pure imagination.

The problems of the heart, considered with reference to the use of the artist, occupied Hawthorne's mind; but one problem in particular had for him an unfailing fascination, — that of the penalty of transgression. Mr. James speaks well of this salient feature, running the tendency back to the grim, Puritan source, and happily expressing the· manner of Hawthorne's escape from the disasters consequent on this line of thought as exhibited by his less fortunate, less artistic ancestors and predecessors. " He contrived," says Mr. James,

" by an exquisite process, best known to himself,
to transmute the heavy moral burden into the
very substance of the imagination, to make it
evaporate in the light and charming fumes of
artistic production." It were hardly safe to
say, however, that had Hawthorne been without
a drop of Puritan blood, he would not have hit
on this dark theme; for it lends itself so readily
to the wonder-working power of the imagina-
tion.   No theme has fastened more firmly on
the mind and heart of man from the call to
Adam in the garden down to the epochal
productions of Dante and Milton.

While Hawthorne's themes are essentially
serious, vital, the treatment develops no more
didacticism than is unobtrusively conveyed by
great art. His convictions are strong, settled.
He had thought and solved for himself as far
perhaps as he deemed it possible or profitable;
but his charming books are of the poet's sort, —
the blossom, not the root, of conviction. In
short, Hawthorne was a teacher only so far as a
master artist is constrained to be.

But imagination does not, of itself, make a great artist; the imagination must be regulated by judgment or taste. If Hawthorne, soaring in his tenuous domain, is never morbid, neither is he made dizzy or confused by his highest flights; indeed, his self-possession is one of the most admirable features of his genius. We have only to compare him with Poe, in this particular, to perceive the advantage of soundness at the core. Be the reader agitated as he may, he feels that the hold of his guide is steady: the guide also is moved, but he will not falter, much less fall in a spasm before the terrors of his own creation. Though the man and the author, or artist, are distinct, Emerson's maxim applies: the great utterance must have a man behind it. Coleridge expresses the same thought when he says that sound sense is at the bottom of all true poetry. Hawthorne was a genuine man, a man with decided peculiarities, but a sane, brainy, full-hearted, earnest man. As has been remarked, he often gives play to light fancies, but even on the sunny sward of elfin merriment is sure to creep the shadow, evincing the sober, brooding mind. The element of restraint includes the sense of humor; and Hawthorne owed much to this sense. Indeed, without it, he, of all authors, would fall short.

The "Scarlet Letter," which lifted Hawthorne to instant fame, was not published until the author was forty-six years old. The "House of the Seven Gables" and the "Blithedale Romance" followed within the next three years. While these three romances exhibit individual excellencies, the public is undoubtedly just in giving the first place to the "Scarlet Letter"; and the space remaining will be devoted to an examination of it in illustration of the working of Hawthorne's mind.

Let this noblest effort of the imagination that America has produced, and one of the most glowing in our language, be introduced in the words of the author himself. Hester is on the scaffold in the Market Place; standing there, awaiting sentence.

" The unhappy culprit sustained herself as best a woman might, under the heavy weight of a thousand unrelenting eyes. . . . Of an impulsive and passionate nature, she had fortified herself to encounter the stings and venemous stabs of public contumely, wreaking itself in every variety of insult; but there was a quality so much more terrible in the solemn mood of the popular mind, that she longed rather to behold all those rigid countenances contorted with scornful merriment, and she herself the object. Had a roar of laughter burst from the multitude, — each man, each woman, each little shrill-voiced child contributing their individual parts, — Hester Prynne might have repaid them all with a bitter, disdainful smile. But, under the leaden infliction which it was her doom to endure, she felt, at moments, as if she must needs shriek out with the full power of her lungs, and cast herself from the scaffold down upon the ground, or else go mad at once."

Never was sensitive, shrinking woman more pitifully placed, the resources of torture are all but exhausted: pressing the babe to her breast, the scene becomes blinding with terror, and for a time her eyes shut against it, while thought reverts to the sweet days of innocence.

" Standing on that miserable eminence, she saw again her native village, in Old England, and her paternal home. She saw her father's face, with its bald brow and reverend white beard that flowed over the old-fashioned Elizabethan ruff; her mother's too, with the look of heedful and anxious love which it always wore in her remembrance, and which, ever since her death, had so often laid the impediment of a gentle remonstrance in her daughter's pathway. She saw her own face, glowing with girlish beauty, and illuminating all the interior of the dusky mirror in which she had been wont to gaze at it."

It would be hard to find the law of contrast working more effectively than in this depiction of the scene before the physical eye and that before the eye of memory. But, dreadful as is the stare of the throng, picture that shape in the midst of it which can make Hester thankful for the vast, cold stare, as a screen against it and its blear organs of vision. She can forget all the other horrors confronting her, at the thought of the near time when she feels she must meet, alone, the old misshapen master of learning, years before made her husband. Thought on this further punishment is interrupted by the voice of a famous young clergyman, seated by the Governor, surrounded by all the pomp of office and by other of her judges, from not one of whom can she hope for the feeblest reach of sympathy. Not so; the situation is worse than that. One word from him whose voice she hears, can draw the iron from her soul, can bid the terrible realities before her fade like the guests of a vision; but the young man, the pale preacher, the idol of his flock, her pastor, her lover, the father of her child, will not utter it. If he speak, it must be, as now, in language even more grievous to bear than his silence.

" ' Hester Prynne,' said he, leaning over the balcony and looking down steadfastly into her eyes, 'thou hearest what this good man says, and seest the accountability under which I labor. If thou feelest it to be for thy soul's peace, and that thy earthly punishment will thereby be made more effectual to salvation, I charge thee to speak out the name of thy fellow-sinner and fellow-sufferer! Be not silent for any mistaken pity and tenderness for him; for, believe me, Hester, though he were to step down from a high place, and stand beside thee on thy pedestal of shame, yet better were it so than to hide a guilty heart through life.' "

The difference between the forlorn woman's understanding of these words and the meaning to the bystanders! we have no more tragic situation in our literature. Pity wavers, for the moment, between the woman, and the man from whom weakness can force such words.

"'Woman, transgress not beyond the limits of Heaven's mercy!' cried the Rev. Mr. Wilson, more harshly than before. . . . 'Speak out the name!' . . .

"'Speak, woman!' said another voice, coldly and sternly, proceeding from the crowd about the scaffold. 'Speak, and give your child a father!'

"'I will not speak!' answered Hester, turning pale as death, but responding to this voice which she too surely recognized."

I will not speak! — these four words atone for a life of sin. The tragic power of this scene far transcends that in Hamlet where the strolling players drive the crowned assassin of buried Denmark beyond the reach of the eager eyes of the dead king's son. Perhaps the chord of pity was never struck more surely: it wakes to endless vibrations.

Later we have woman in her mother's

strength, when, at the Governor's Hall, stern
men threaten to take from her all that is left,
her child. Fettered by fidelity to her masked
lover, she will not betray the father; but their
child must not be wrenched from her breast.

"'God gave her into my keeping,' repeated
Hester Prynne, raising her voice almost to a
shriek. 'I will not give her up!' And here,
by a sudden impulse, she turned to the young
clergyman, Mr. Dimmesdale, at whom, up to
this moment, she had seemed hardly so much as
to raise her eyes. 'Speak thou for me!' cried
she. 'Thou wast my pastor, and hadst charge
of my soul, and knowest me better than these
men can. I will not lose the child! Speak for
me! Thou knowest — for thou hast sympathies
which these men lack! — thou knowest what is
in my heart, and what are a mother's rights,
and how much stronger they are when that
mother has but her child and the scarlet
letter!'"

It is not in the power of human nature to

long endure the strain of such concealment as the Rev. Dimmesdale's. In the damp, cold, dark night, he gropes his way to the fateful scaffold, mounts it, and stands, a statue, till his limbs begin to grow rigid beneath him. Though the victory is incomplete, remorse has given fierce battle to cowardice. Hester passes, on her way home from watching at a death-bed.

"'Come up hither, Hester, thou and little Pearl,' said the Rev. Mr. Dimmesdale. 'Ye have both been here before, but I was not with you. Come up hither once again, and we will stand all three together.'"

As they stand there, in the darkness of the night, pathos reaches its limit in the pleading of little Pearl, now come to girlhood, that the clergyman will stand in the same dread place with her mother and herself to-morrow noon-tide.

Listen to the clergymen when, at last, covered with the honors of a festal day, he steps from the admiring procession, once more to ascend the scaffold. Remorse has now finished the fight, won the victory, and he appears on the pedestal of shame between Hester Prynne and little Pearl.

"'People of New England, . . . ye that have loved me! ye that have deemed me holy! behold me here, the one sinner of the world. . . . Now, at the death hour, he stands up before you. . . . Stand any here that question God's judgment on a sinner? Behold! Behold a dreadful witness of it!'"

The repentant transgressor forgives his persecutor, kisses his little Pearl, bids farewell to Hester, and sinks rapidly into unconsciousness. Has the wretched man purchased peace at last, may he hope; and what of her he leaves behind? Hawthorne does not omit this last touch with which to complete the desolation. "'Shall we not meet again?' whispers Hester, bending her face down close to his. 'Shall we not spend our immortal life together? Surely, surely, we have ransomed one another, with all this woe! Thou lookest far into eternity with those bright, dying eyes! Then tell me what thou seest.'

" ' Hester, Hester, . . . I fear! I fear! ' "

Hester's last words to the dying man move depths untouched by Charoba over the body of Gebir, the king, wedded and lost in the same hour. This scene, on and about the scaffold of the bleak New England town, was much more like that at

> . . . "the feast of Cepheus, when the sword
> Of Phineus, white with wonder, shook restrained,
> And the hilt rattled in his marble hand."

We have said that Hawthorne's characters are personified forces of the human mind and heart. Old Roger Chillingsworth, in the disguise of an injured husband seeking revenge, is really the Rev. Mr. Dimmesdale's guilty conscience incarnate. He follows the clergyman stealthily, steadily, sure as death itself of his prey. Hawthorne is rarely, if ever, more subtile than in the quiet but fierce contest between these two men : such strokes and parries are possible only to consummate art. After the discovery of the fatal sign on the preacher's bared breast, the old man's malice increases rapidly, and he soon becomes a very devil. The inevitable result of Chillingsworth's incessant goading — the gnawing of conscience — is a weakening of his victim's manhood. This Hester must perceive ; and once more woman's strength towers over mountainous calamity, infusing the drooping man with courage and hope. It is the same strange might of woman, when too far driven, that, turned into a wicked channel, could shake with its terrible tongue the frame of valiant Macbeth.

In passing, if Hester reminds us of Lady Macbeth, the Rev. Mr. Dimmesdale reminds us more strongly of Hamlet. A clew to Hawthorne's order of thought is found in his frequent suggestion of parallels with Shakespeare, and few with other writers.

The "Scarlet Letter," is so saturated with
pathos that the least lovable character in it
makes a heavy demand upon pity. The words
of hoary Roger Chillingsworth to Hester in
the prison, have the old Hebraic ring, insuring
immediate sympathy : —

"'One thing, thou that wast my wife, I
would enjoin upon thee. Thou hast kept the
secret of thy paramour. Keep, likewise, mine!
There are none in this land that know me.
Breathe not to any human soul, that thou didst
ever call me husband! Here, on this wild
outskirt of the earth, I shall pitch my tent;
for, elsewhere, a wanderer, and isolated from
human interests, I find here a woman, a man,
and a child, amongst whom and myself there
exist the closest ligaments. No matter whether
of love or hate ; no matter whether of right or
wrong! thou and thine, Hester Prynne, belong
to me. My home is where thou art, and *where
he is*. But betray me not!'"

Here again, in the words we have italicized,

is that last touch which only the subtilest genius can give.

As for Hester's long, dreary after-years amidst the prejudice and scorn of the Puritan settlement — Hagar herself, with her babe in the wilderness, did not know so awful a solitude. Little Pearl inspires the same unfailing sentiment of commiseration. In the picturing of Pearl, who is no other than the personified sweet of pleasure touched with the bitterness of bliss forbidden, Hawthorne puts his nimble fancy into a frock, giving it a pair of bright, black eyes, and shining curls. Her elfin dance over the grass — that is Hawthorne's airy thought at play on soberest ground.

As before observed, one of the elemental charms of Hawthorne's pictures is the background of nature. Faithful to nature, still he exercises in the highest degree the artist's privilege, touching in his own light and shade, adding the enchanting atmosphere of imagination. Compare the nature in the "Forest Walk," where Pearl asks her mother about the Black Man, with the nature in the scene where Hester's life-load is for the moment lifted by the Rev. Mr. Dimmesdale's consent to escape with her. The natural objects are much the same, but their expression changes, like that of a human face, in sympathy with the emotions to which they are mute ministers. This is the poet's method of dealing with nature — a signal excellence, for example, of Tennyson's verse — the method that evidences the creative power, that betokens the excelling gift of imagination.

As a student of the human heart, Hawthorne is eminently successful in what is deemed the last conquest — the mastery of the heart of woman. Hester, utterly abandoned, unable to gain entrance to the church because of the crowd, stands on the outside, by the scaffold, to catch the *accent* of the Rev. Mr. Dimmesdale's tones as he proceeds in his marvellous discourse. " Muffled as the sound was, by its passage through the church walls, Hester Prynne listened with such intentness, and sympathized so intimately, that the sermon had throughout a meaning for her, *entirely apart from its distinguishable words.*"

This revelation of woman's nature, is obviously of a very different school from the fastidious, cuticular school which informs us, perchance, whether a woman puts out a match with a puff of breath or by flourishing it in her fingers.

In the course of Hawthorne's steady probing into the secrets of the passions, we continually meet with startling suggestions; such as the possible identity, at bottom, of love and hate. Another peculiarity is the deft stroke by which scene and incident are invested with a haunting quality. After Hester's refusal to betray the partner of her guilt, what happened as she passed back into her cell?

" It was whispered by those who peered after

her, that the scarlet letter threw a lurid
gleam along the dark passage-way of the in-
terior."

To find that touch again, we must go back to
the " Ancient Mariner," to " Christabel." And
who but Hawthorne would have hit on the
device of making poor, persecuted Hester look
into the convex mirror of the polished breast-
plate hanging in the Governor's Hall, there to
see with the physical eye the letter, frightfully
magnified, that was perpetually reflected from
all faces and things inanimate upon her spirit-
ual sight?

It is hardly necessary to add that success,
such as Hawthorne's, implies the happiest ex-
pression. Not to dwell on Hawthorne's style,
simple mention may be made of his power of
condensation, his exquisite application of the
law of contrast, his repose, his judgment or
taste ; and, over and above all, his poet's skill in
suggestiveness and in the creation of atmos-
phere, his primal power of pure, bold, sustained

imagination — imagination which, for purity
and subtilty has been equalled in English
literature perhaps not more than once before
since the robe fell from the shoulders of the
unapproachable Elizabethan.